50 Kansas City Barbecue Recipes for Home

By: Kelly Johnson

Table of Contents

- Kansas City-style Barbecue Ribs
- Burnt Ends
- Kansas City Brisket
- BBQ Pulled Pork Sandwiches
- Smoked Chicken Wings
- BBQ Baked Beans
- BBQ Beef Burnt Ends
- Kansas City BBQ Sauce
- Smoked Pork Belly
- BBQ Chicken Thighs
- BBQ Pork Spare Ribs
- Grilled Corn on the Cob with BBQ Butter
- Smoked Turkey Breast
- BBQ Meatloaf
- Smoked Sausages with BBQ Sauce
- BBQ Pork Shoulder
- Kansas City Rib Tips
- Smoked Beef Brisket Sandwiches
- BBQ Pulled Chicken
- BBQ Stuffed Jalapeños
- BBQ Mac and Cheese
- Smoked Pork Chops
- BBQ Potato Salad
- Kansas City-style Burnt Ends Chili
- Smoked Beef Short Ribs
- BBQ Coleslaw
- BBQ Chicken Skewers
- Smoked Pork Loin
- BBQ Beef Brisket Burnt Ends
- Smoked Chicken Thighs
- BBQ Pulled Pork Nachos
- Kansas City BBQ Baked Potato
- Smoked Beef Ribs
- BBQ Bacon-wrapped Shrimp
- BBQ Pulled Pork Pizza

- Smoked Turkey Legs
- Kansas City BBQ Beef Sandwiches
- BBQ Stuffed Bell Peppers
- BBQ Chicken Pizza
- Smoked Sausage and Pepper Skewers
- BBQ Pulled Pork Tacos
- Kansas City BBQ Sliders
- Smoked BBQ Meatballs
- BBQ Chicken Drumsticks
- BBQ Pork Belly Burnt Ends
- Kansas City BBQ Beef Ribs
- Smoked BBQ Chicken Salad
- BBQ Pork Tenderloin
- Kansas City BBQ Chicken Wings
- BBQ Beef Brisket Tacos

Kansas City-style Barbecue Ribs

Ingredients:

- 2 racks of pork ribs (baby back or St. Louis-style)
- 1 cup Kansas City-style barbecue sauce (store-bought or homemade)
- Dry Rub:
    - 1/4 cup brown sugar
    - 2 tablespoons paprika
    - 1 tablespoon garlic powder
    - 1 tablespoon onion powder
    - 1 tablespoon chili powder
    - 1 tablespoon ground cumin
    - 1 tablespoon black pepper
    - 1 teaspoon salt

Instructions:

1. Prepare the Ribs:
    - Remove the membrane from the back of the ribs. Use a butter knife to loosen it, then grab it with a paper towel and pull it off.
    - Pat the ribs dry with paper towels.
2. Apply the Dry Rub:
    - In a small bowl, mix together all the dry rub ingredients until well combined.
    - Rub the dry rub mixture all over the ribs, covering them evenly. Use your hands to massage the rub into the meat.
    - Wrap the ribs in plastic wrap and refrigerate for at least 2 hours, or overnight if possible, to allow the flavors to penetrate the meat.
3. Preheat the Grill:
    - Preheat your grill to medium heat (about 275-300°F). Set it up for indirect cooking by turning off one burner or arranging the coals to one side, so the ribs can cook over indirect heat.
4. Grill the Ribs:
    - Place the ribs on the grill over indirect heat, bone-side down.
    - Close the lid and cook for 2-3 hours, or until the ribs are tender and the meat has pulled back from the bones. You can check for doneness by inserting a toothpick between the bones; it should slide in easily.

- During the last 30 minutes of cooking, brush the ribs with Kansas City-style barbecue sauce, applying several coats and allowing each layer to caramelize slightly before adding the next.
5. Rest and Serve:
    - Once the ribs are done, remove them from the grill and let them rest for 10-15 minutes before slicing.
    - Slice the ribs between the bones and serve with extra barbecue sauce on the side.
6. Enjoy:
    - Serve your Kansas City-style barbecue ribs with your favorite sides, such as coleslaw, cornbread, baked beans, or potato salad.
    - Enjoy the smoky, sweet, and savory flavors of these delicious ribs!

This recipe yields tender and flavorful ribs with a perfect balance of smokiness and sweetness, typical of Kansas City-style barbecue.

Burnt Ends

Ingredients:

- 1 whole beef brisket (about 10-12 pounds)
- Your favorite dry rub seasoning
- Barbecue sauce (optional)
- Wood chips or chunks for smoking (hickory or oak work well)

Instructions:

1. Prepare the Brisket:
    - Trim any excess fat from the brisket, leaving about 1/4 inch of fat on the surface.
    - Season the brisket generously with your favorite dry rub seasoning, covering all sides of the meat. Let it sit at room temperature for about 30 minutes while you prepare the smoker.
2. Preheat the Smoker:
    - Preheat your smoker to 225-250°F (107-121°C). Use hickory or oak wood chips or chunks for smoking, as they provide a rich flavor that complements the beef.
3. Smoke the Brisket:
    - Place the seasoned brisket in the smoker, fat side up, and close the lid.
    - Smoke the brisket for 10-12 hours, or until it reaches an internal temperature of 195-205°F (91-96°C) and is tender and easily pierced with a probe or fork.
4. Slice and Cube the Brisket:
    - Once the brisket is done, remove it from the smoker and let it rest for about 20-30 minutes.
    - Slice the brisket against the grain into 1-inch slices, then cube the slices into bite-sized pieces.
5. Make the Burnt Ends:
    - Place the cubed brisket pieces in a disposable aluminum pan or a baking dish.
    - If desired, toss the burnt end cubes with your favorite barbecue sauce to coat them evenly.
    - Return the pan to the smoker and continue cooking for an additional 1-2 hours, or until the burnt ends are caramelized and have a slightly crispy exterior.
6. Serve and Enjoy:

- Once the burnt ends are done, remove them from the smoker and let them cool slightly.
- Serve the burnt ends as a delicious appetizer, sandwich filling, or main dish, alongside your favorite barbecue sides such as coleslaw, baked beans, or potato salad.
- Enjoy the rich, smoky flavor and melt-in-your-mouth tenderness of these irresistible burnt ends!

With their caramelized exterior and tender interior, burnt ends are a true barbecue delicacy that will impress your guests and leave them craving more.

Kansas City Brisket

Ingredients:

- 1 whole beef brisket (10-12 pounds)
- Your favorite dry rub seasoning
- Wood chips or chunks for smoking (hickory or oak work well)
- Barbecue sauce (optional, for serving)

Instructions:

1. Prepare the Brisket:
    - Trim any excess fat from the brisket, leaving about 1/4 inch of fat on the surface.
    - Season the brisket generously with your favorite dry rub seasoning, covering all sides of the meat. Let it sit at room temperature for about 30 minutes while you prepare the smoker.
2. Preheat the Smoker:
    - Preheat your smoker to 225-250°F (107-121°C). Use hickory or oak wood chips or chunks for smoking, as they provide a rich flavor that complements the beef.
3. Smoke the Brisket:
    - Place the seasoned brisket in the smoker, fat side up, and close the lid.
    - Smoke the brisket for 10-12 hours, or until it reaches an internal temperature of 195-205°F (91-96°C) and is tender and easily pierced with a probe or fork.
4. Rest the Brisket:
    - Once the brisket is done, remove it from the smoker and wrap it tightly in butcher paper or aluminum foil.
    - Let the brisket rest for at least 1 hour to allow the juices to redistribute and the meat to become even more tender.
5. Slice and Serve:
    - Unwrap the brisket and transfer it to a cutting board.
    - Slice the brisket against the grain into thin slices, about 1/4 to 1/2 inch thick.
    - Serve the sliced brisket with your favorite barbecue sauce on the side, if desired.
6. Enjoy:
    - Serve the Kansas City brisket with classic barbecue sides such as coleslaw, baked beans, cornbread, or potato salad.

- Enjoy the rich, smoky flavor and melt-in-your-mouth tenderness of this iconic barbecue dish with family and friends.

With its perfect balance of smoky flavor and tender texture, Kansas City brisket is sure to be a hit at your next barbecue gathering.

BBQ Pulled Pork Sandwiches

Ingredients:

- 3-4 pounds pork shoulder (also known as pork butt)
- 1 tablespoon olive oil
- 1 onion, diced
- 3 cloves garlic, minced
- 1 cup barbecue sauce, plus extra for serving
- 1/2 cup chicken or vegetable broth
- 1 tablespoon brown sugar
- 1 tablespoon Worcestershire sauce
- 1 teaspoon smoked paprika
- 1 teaspoon chili powder
- 1/2 teaspoon ground cumin
- Salt and pepper, to taste
- Hamburger buns or sandwich rolls, for serving
- Coleslaw, for topping (optional)

Instructions:

1. Preheat the Oven:
    - Preheat your oven to 325°F (163°C).
2. Prepare the Pork Shoulder:
    - Trim any excess fat from the pork shoulder, then season it generously with salt and pepper.
    - In a large Dutch oven or oven-safe pot, heat the olive oil over medium-high heat. Add the pork shoulder and sear it on all sides until browned, about 3-4 minutes per side. Remove the pork from the pot and set it aside.
3. Sauté the Onions and Garlic:
    - In the same pot, add the diced onions and minced garlic. Sauté until softened and fragrant, about 3-4 minutes.
4. Make the BBQ Sauce Mixture:
    - Add the barbecue sauce, chicken or vegetable broth, brown sugar, Worcestershire sauce, smoked paprika, chili powder, and ground cumin to the pot. Stir well to combine.
5. Cook the Pork:
    - Return the seared pork shoulder to the pot, nestling it into the barbecue sauce mixture.
    - Cover the pot with a lid and transfer it to the preheated oven.

- Bake the pork shoulder for 3-4 hours, or until it is tender and easily shreds with a fork.
6. Shred the Pork:
    - Once the pork is done cooking, remove it from the oven and transfer it to a cutting board.
    - Use two forks to shred the pork into bite-sized pieces, discarding any excess fat.
7. Finish the Sauce:
    - If desired, skim off any excess fat from the surface of the barbecue sauce in the pot.
    - Use an immersion blender or transfer the sauce to a blender to puree until smooth. Alternatively, you can leave the sauce chunky, depending on your preference.
8. Combine the Pork and Sauce:
    - Return the shredded pork to the pot with the barbecue sauce, stirring until the pork is evenly coated.
9. Assemble the Sandwiches:
    - To serve, spoon the BBQ pulled pork onto hamburger buns or sandwich rolls.
    - Top with additional barbecue sauce, if desired, and coleslaw for added crunch and flavor.
10. Enjoy:
    - Serve the BBQ pulled pork sandwiches immediately, accompanied by your favorite sides such as potato chips, pickles, or a fresh green salad.
    - Enjoy the irresistible combination of tender, smoky pulled pork and tangy barbecue sauce in every bite!

These BBQ pulled pork sandwiches are sure to be a hit at your next gathering or family meal. They're easy to make and packed with flavor, making them a crowd-pleasing favorite.

Smoked Chicken Wings

Ingredients:

- 2-3 pounds chicken wings, split at the joint and tips removed
- Your favorite dry rub seasoning
- Barbecue sauce (optional, for serving)

For the Brine (optional):

- 4 cups cold water
- 1/4 cup kosher salt
- 1/4 cup brown sugar
- 2 cloves garlic, smashed
- 1 tablespoon whole black peppercorns
- 1 lemon, sliced

Instructions:

1. Brine the Chicken Wings (optional):
    - In a large bowl or container, combine the water, kosher salt, brown sugar, smashed garlic cloves, black peppercorns, and lemon slices. Stir until the salt and sugar are dissolved.
    - Add the chicken wings to the brine, making sure they are fully submerged. Cover and refrigerate for 1-2 hours (or up to 4 hours for a stronger brine flavor).
2. Prepare the Smoker:
    - Preheat your smoker to 225-250°F (107-121°C). Use wood chips or chunks for smoking; applewood, hickory, or cherry wood are great options for chicken.
3. Season the Chicken Wings:
    - Remove the chicken wings from the brine and pat them dry with paper towels.
    - Season the wings generously with your favorite dry rub seasoning, coating them evenly on all sides.
4. Smoke the Chicken Wings:
    - Arrange the seasoned chicken wings on the smoker rack, leaving space between each wing for the smoke to circulate.

- Close the smoker lid and smoke the wings for 1.5 to 2 hours, or until they reach an internal temperature of 165°F (74°C) and the skin is crispy and golden brown.
- Optionally, you can baste the wings with barbecue sauce during the last 15-20 minutes of smoking for added flavor.

5. Serve and Enjoy:
    - Once the smoked chicken wings are done, remove them from the smoker and let them rest for a few minutes.
    - Serve the wings hot with your favorite dipping sauce or additional barbecue sauce on the side.
    - Enjoy the smoky, tender, and flavorful goodness of these irresistible smoked chicken wings with friends and family!

These smoked chicken wings are sure to be a hit at any gathering or barbecue, with their juicy meat, crispy skin, and mouthwatering barbecue flavor. Serve them as an appetizer or main dish, and watch them disappear in no time!

BBQ Baked Beans

Ingredients:

- 4 cans (15 ounces each) of your favorite canned baked beans (such as navy beans or pinto beans)
- 1/2 cup barbecue sauce
- 1/4 cup ketchup
- 1/4 cup brown sugar
- 2 tablespoons yellow mustard
- 1 tablespoon Worcestershire sauce
- 1 small onion, finely diced
- 4 slices of bacon, chopped
- Salt and pepper to taste

Instructions:

1. Preheat the Oven:
   - Preheat your oven to 350°F (175°C).
2. Prepare the Beans:
   - Drain and rinse the canned baked beans in a colander. This helps to remove excess salt and liquid.
3. Cook the Bacon and Onion:
   - In a large skillet, cook the chopped bacon over medium heat until it starts to crisp up, about 5-7 minutes.
   - Add the diced onion to the skillet with the bacon and cook until the onion is soft and translucent, about 3-4 minutes more. Remove from heat.
4. Combine the Ingredients:
   - In a large mixing bowl, combine the drained baked beans, barbecue sauce, ketchup, brown sugar, yellow mustard, Worcestershire sauce, cooked bacon, and onion. Stir well to combine all the ingredients.
5. Season and Adjust:
   - Taste the BBQ baked beans mixture and season with salt and pepper to taste. You can also adjust the sweetness or tanginess by adding more brown sugar or mustard, according to your preference.
6. Bake the Beans:
   - Transfer the BBQ baked beans mixture to a 9x13-inch baking dish or a similar-sized oven-safe dish.
   - Cover the dish with aluminum foil and bake in the preheated oven for 45-60 minutes, or until the beans are bubbly and the sauce has thickened.

7. Serve and Enjoy:
   - Once the BBQ baked beans are done baking, remove them from the oven and let them cool slightly before serving.
   - Serve the beans hot as a side dish alongside your favorite barbecue meats, burgers, or hot dogs.
   - Enjoy the rich, smoky, and savory flavor of these homemade BBQ baked beans with family and friends!

These BBQ baked beans are sure to be a hit at any cookout or gathering, with their sweet, tangy, and savory flavors complementing a variety of grilled and barbecued dishes. Plus, they're easy to make and can be prepared in advance, making them a convenient side dish for any occasion.

BBQ Beef Burnt Ends

Ingredients:

- 4-5 pounds beef brisket point (also known as the deckle or fatty end)
- Your favorite dry rub seasoning
- Barbecue sauce
- Honey (optional, for glazing)

Instructions:

1. Prepare the Brisket:
    - Trim any excess fat from the surface of the brisket point, leaving a thin layer for flavor and moisture retention.
    - Season the brisket point generously with your favorite dry rub seasoning, covering all sides of the meat. Let it sit at room temperature for about 30 minutes while you prepare the smoker.
2. Preheat the Smoker:
    - Preheat your smoker to 225-250°F (107-121°C). Use wood chips or chunks for smoking; hickory, oak, or pecan wood work well for beef.
3. Smoke the Brisket Point:
    - Place the seasoned brisket point on the smoker rack, fat side up, and close the lid.
    - Smoke the brisket point for 6-8 hours, or until it reaches an internal temperature of 195-205°F (91-96°C) and is tender and easily pierced with a probe or fork.
4. Rest and Cube the Brisket:
    - Once the brisket point is done smoking, remove it from the smoker and let it rest for about 20-30 minutes.
    - Use a sharp knife to cube the brisket point into bite-sized pieces, about 1 to 1.5 inches wide.
5. Toss in BBQ Sauce:
    - Place the cubed brisket pieces in a disposable aluminum pan or a baking dish.
    - Pour your favorite barbecue sauce over the cubed brisket, tossing to coat the pieces evenly.
6. Return to the Smoker:
    - Return the pan of cubed brisket to the smoker and continue cooking for an additional 1-2 hours, or until the burnt ends are caramelized and have a slightly crispy exterior.

7. Optional Glazing:
   - If desired, you can glaze the burnt ends with honey during the last 15-20 minutes of cooking for added sweetness and shine.
8. Serve and Enjoy:
   - Once the BBQ beef burnt ends are done, remove them from the smoker and let them cool slightly.
   - Serve the burnt ends hot as a delicious appetizer, sandwich filling, or main dish, alongside your favorite barbecue sides.
   - Enjoy the rich, smoky flavor and melt-in-your-mouth tenderness of these irresistible BBQ beef burnt ends with family and friends!

These BBQ beef burnt ends are sure to be a hit at your next barbecue gathering, with their caramelized exterior, tender interior, and mouthwatering barbecue flavor. Serve them as a standalone dish or incorporate them into sandwiches, tacos, or salads for added versatility.

Kansas City BBQ Sauce

Ingredients:

- 2 cups ketchup
- 1/2 cup apple cider vinegar
- 1/2 cup brown sugar
- 1/4 cup molasses
- 2 tablespoons Worcestershire sauce
- 1 tablespoon yellow mustard
- 1 tablespoon smoked paprika
- 1 teaspoon garlic powder
- 1 teaspoon onion powder
- 1/2 teaspoon cayenne pepper (adjust to taste for spiciness)
- Salt and black pepper to taste

Instructions:

1. Combine Ingredients:
    - In a medium saucepan, combine the ketchup, apple cider vinegar, brown sugar, molasses, Worcestershire sauce, yellow mustard, smoked paprika, garlic powder, onion powder, and cayenne pepper.
2. Simmer Sauce:
    - Place the saucepan over medium heat and stir to combine all the ingredients.
    - Bring the mixture to a simmer, then reduce the heat to low. Let the sauce simmer gently for 20-30 minutes, stirring occasionally, to allow the flavors to meld and the sauce to thicken slightly.
3. Adjust Seasoning:
    - Taste the BBQ sauce and adjust the seasoning as needed. Add salt and black pepper to taste, and adjust the level of cayenne pepper for spiciness according to your preference.
4. Cool and Store:
    - Once the BBQ sauce has reached your desired consistency and flavor, remove it from the heat and let it cool to room temperature.
    - Transfer the cooled BBQ sauce to a clean jar or airtight container for storage. It can be stored in the refrigerator for up to 2 weeks.
5. Serve and Enjoy:

- Use the Kansas City BBQ sauce as a marinade, basting sauce, or dipping sauce for a variety of barbecue dishes such as ribs, pulled pork, brisket, chicken, or grilled vegetables.
- Enjoy the rich, tangy, and slightly sweet flavor of this homemade Kansas City-style BBQ sauce with your favorite barbecue creations!

This homemade Kansas City BBQ sauce is sure to elevate your barbecue game with its delicious flavor and versatility. Adjust the seasonings to suit your taste preferences and enjoy the authentic taste of Kansas City barbecue in the comfort of your own home.

Smoked Pork Belly

Ingredients:

- 2-3 pounds pork belly, skin removed
- Your favorite dry rub seasoning
- Wood chips or chunks for smoking (applewood, hickory, or oak work well)

Instructions:

1. Prepare the Pork Belly:
   - If the pork belly still has the skin on, use a sharp knife to remove it, leaving behind the layer of fat.
   - Pat the pork belly dry with paper towels.
2. Apply the Dry Rub:
   - Season the pork belly generously with your favorite dry rub seasoning, covering all sides of the meat. You can use a pre-made dry rub or create your own blend of spices.
3. Preheat the Smoker:
   - Preheat your smoker to 225-250°F (107-121°C). Use wood chips or chunks for smoking; applewood, hickory, or oak wood impart excellent flavor to pork belly.
4. Smoke the Pork Belly:
   - Place the seasoned pork belly on the smoker rack, fat side up, and close the lid.
   - Smoke the pork belly for 3-4 hours, or until it reaches an internal temperature of 195-200°F (91-93°C) and the meat is tender and juicy.
5. Rest and Slice:
   - Once the pork belly is done smoking, remove it from the smoker and let it rest for about 10-15 minutes.
   - Use a sharp knife to slice the smoked pork belly into thick slices or cubes, depending on your preference.
6. Serve and Enjoy:
   - Serve the smoked pork belly slices as a delicious appetizer, main dish, or topping for salads, sandwiches, or tacos.
   - Enjoy the rich, smoky flavor and melt-in-your-mouth tenderness of this irresistible smoked pork belly with family and friends!

Smoked pork belly is a versatile dish that can be enjoyed on its own or incorporated into a variety of recipes. Whether served as a main course or used to add flavor to other dishes, smoked pork belly is sure to be a hit with barbecue enthusiasts and food lovers alike.

BBQ Chicken Thighs

Ingredients:

- 8 bone-in, skin-on chicken thighs
- Your favorite BBQ dry rub seasoning
- BBQ sauce (optional, for basting and serving)

Instructions:

1. Prepare the Chicken Thighs:
    - Rinse the chicken thighs under cold water and pat them dry with paper towels.
    - Trim any excess skin or fat if desired.
2. Season the Chicken Thighs:
    - Season the chicken thighs generously with your favorite BBQ dry rub seasoning, covering all sides of the meat. You can use a store-bought rub or make your own blend of spices.
3. Preheat the Grill:
    - Preheat your grill to medium-high heat, around 375-400°F (190-204°C). If using a charcoal grill, arrange the coals for indirect cooking.
4. Grill the Chicken Thighs:
    - Place the seasoned chicken thighs on the preheated grill, skin side down, over direct heat.
    - Grill the chicken thighs for 5-6 minutes on each side, or until the skin is golden brown and crispy, and the internal temperature reaches 165°F (74°C) when measured with a meat thermometer.
5. Baste with BBQ Sauce (Optional):
    - If desired, baste the chicken thighs with BBQ sauce during the last few minutes of grilling, turning them occasionally to prevent burning. This will add extra flavor and caramelization to the chicken.
6. Rest and Serve:
    - Once the chicken thighs are cooked through and the skin is crispy, remove them from the grill and let them rest for a few minutes before serving.
    - Serve the BBQ chicken thighs hot, with additional BBQ sauce on the side if desired.
7. Enjoy:
    - Enjoy the tender, juicy, and flavorful BBQ chicken thighs as a main dish or alongside your favorite barbecue sides, such as coleslaw, baked beans, or cornbread.

BBQ chicken thighs are a delicious and crowd-pleasing option for any barbecue or cookout. With their smoky flavor and succulent meat, they're sure to become a favorite on your grill menu.

BBQ Pork Spare Ribs

Ingredients:

- 2 racks of pork spare ribs (about 4-5 pounds total)
- Your favorite dry rub seasoning
- BBQ sauce (optional, for basting and serving)

Instructions:

1. Prepare the Ribs:
    - Remove the membrane from the back of the ribs. Use a butter knife to loosen it, then grab it with a paper towel and pull it off.
    - Trim any excess fat from the ribs, if desired.
    - Pat the ribs dry with paper towels.
2. Season the Ribs:
    - Season the ribs generously with your favorite dry rub seasoning, covering all sides of the meat. You can use a store-bought rub or make your own blend of spices.
3. Preheat the Grill:
    - Preheat your grill to 225-250°F (107-121°C). Set it up for indirect cooking by turning off one burner or arranging the coals to one side, so the ribs can cook over indirect heat.
4. Smoke the Ribs:
    - Place the seasoned ribs on the grill, bone-side down, over indirect heat.
    - Close the lid and let the ribs smoke for 3-4 hours, or until they are tender and the meat has pulled back from the bones. You can check for doneness by inserting a toothpick between the bones; it should slide in easily.
5. Baste with BBQ Sauce (Optional):
    - If desired, baste the ribs with BBQ sauce during the last 30 minutes of cooking, applying several coats and allowing each layer to caramelize slightly before adding the next.
6. Rest and Serve:
    - Once the ribs are done, remove them from the grill and let them rest for 10-15 minutes before slicing.
    - Slice the ribs between the bones and serve with extra BBQ sauce on the side.
7. Enjoy:

- Serve the BBQ pork spare ribs hot, with your favorite barbecue sides such as coleslaw, baked beans, or cornbread.
- Enjoy the tender, smoky, and flavorful BBQ pork spare ribs with family and friends!

With their melt-in-your-mouth tenderness and rich flavor, BBQ pork spare ribs are sure to be a hit at your next barbecue gathering. Plus, they're easy to make and can be customized with your favorite dry rub and BBQ sauce for a personalized touch.

Grilled Corn on the Cob with BBQ Butter

Ingredients:

- 4 ears of corn, husks removed
- 1/2 cup unsalted butter, softened
- 2 tablespoons barbecue sauce
- 1 teaspoon smoked paprika
- 1/2 teaspoon garlic powder
- Salt and pepper to taste
- Fresh parsley or chives, chopped (for garnish)

Instructions:

1. Preheat the Grill:
    - Preheat your grill to medium-high heat, around 375-400°F (190-204°C).
2. Prepare the BBQ Butter:
    - In a small bowl, combine the softened butter, barbecue sauce, smoked paprika, garlic powder, salt, and pepper. Mix until well combined.
3. Grill the Corn:
    - Place the ears of corn directly on the grill grates.
    - Grill the corn for 10-15 minutes, turning occasionally, until the kernels are tender and lightly charred in spots.
4. Apply the BBQ Butter:
    - Remove the corn from the grill and transfer it to a serving platter.
    - While the corn is still hot, spread the BBQ butter generously over each ear, using a spoon or pastry brush to coat them evenly.
5. Garnish and Serve:
    - Sprinkle the grilled corn with chopped parsley or chives for a pop of color and freshness.
    - Serve the corn on the cob hot as a delicious side dish or accompaniment to grilled meats, seafood, or other barbecue favorites.
6. Enjoy:
    - Sink your teeth into the juicy, smoky-sweet kernels of corn, enhanced by the rich and flavorful BBQ butter. It's a perfect combination of summertime flavors that will have everyone coming back for seconds!

Grilled corn on the cob with BBQ butter is a simple yet impressive dish that's sure to be a hit at any barbecue or summer gathering. The savory, tangy flavors of the BBQ butter complement the natural sweetness of the corn, creating a mouthwatering treat that's perfect for warm weather dining.

Smoked Turkey Breast

Ingredients:

- 1 bone-in turkey breast (about 4-6 pounds)
- Your favorite poultry dry rub seasoning
- Wood chips or chunks for smoking (applewood, hickory, or cherry wood work well)
- Olive oil or melted butter for basting (optional)

Instructions:

1. Prepare the Turkey Breast:
    - Rinse the turkey breast under cold water and pat it dry with paper towels.
    - If there's excess skin or fat, trim it off, leaving a thin layer for flavor and moisture.
2. Season the Turkey Breast:
    - Rub the turkey breast generously with your favorite poultry dry rub seasoning, covering all sides of the meat. You can use a store-bought rub or make your own blend of herbs and spices.
3. Preheat the Smoker:
    - Preheat your smoker to 225-250°F (107-121°C). Use wood chips or chunks for smoking; applewood, hickory, or cherry wood are excellent choices for poultry.
4. Smoke the Turkey Breast:
    - Place the seasoned turkey breast on the smoker rack, skin side up, and close the lid.
    - Smoke the turkey breast for approximately 30-40 minutes per pound, or until it reaches an internal temperature of 165°F (74°C) when measured with a meat thermometer inserted into the thickest part of the breast.
5. Baste with Olive Oil or Butter (Optional):
    - If desired, baste the turkey breast with olive oil or melted butter every hour during the smoking process to keep the meat moist and enhance its flavor.
6. Rest and Serve:
    - Once the turkey breast is done smoking, remove it from the smoker and let it rest for 15-20 minutes before slicing.
    - Slice the smoked turkey breast thinly against the grain and arrange the slices on a serving platter.
7. Enjoy:

- Serve the smoked turkey breast hot as a delicious main dish or sliced cold for sandwiches, salads, or wraps.
- Enjoy the rich, smoky flavor and juicy tenderness of this homemade smoked turkey breast with your favorite sides and condiments.

Smoked turkey breast is a flavorful and versatile dish that's sure to be a hit with family and friends. Whether served hot or cold, it's a delicious addition to any meal or gathering, and the leftovers are perfect for enjoying in a variety of dishes throughout the week.

BBQ Meatloaf

Ingredients:

- 1 1/2 pounds ground beef (or a mixture of beef and pork)
- 1 small onion, finely diced
- 2 cloves garlic, minced
- 1/2 cup breadcrumbs
- 1/4 cup milk
- 1/4 cup barbecue sauce, plus extra for glazing
- 1 large egg
- 1 teaspoon Worcestershire sauce
- 1 teaspoon dried oregano
- 1 teaspoon dried parsley
- Salt and pepper to taste

For Glazing:

- Additional barbecue sauce

Instructions:

1. Preheat the Oven:
   - Preheat your oven to 350°F (175°C).
2. Mix the Ingredients:
   - In a large mixing bowl, combine the ground beef, diced onion, minced garlic, breadcrumbs, milk, barbecue sauce, egg, Worcestershire sauce, dried oregano, dried parsley, salt, and pepper. Mix until all ingredients are well combined.
3. Shape the Meatloaf:
   - Transfer the meat mixture to a baking dish or a loaf pan, shaping it into a loaf shape.
4. Bake the Meatloaf:
   - Place the meatloaf in the preheated oven and bake for 40-45 minutes, or until the internal temperature reaches 160°F (71°C) when measured with a meat thermometer.
5. Glaze the Meatloaf:
   - Remove the meatloaf from the oven and brush the top with additional barbecue sauce for added flavor and moisture.
6. Finish Baking:

- Return the meatloaf to the oven and continue baking for an additional 10-15 minutes, or until the barbecue sauce glaze is sticky and caramelized.
7. Rest and Serve:
    - Once the meatloaf is done baking, remove it from the oven and let it rest for a few minutes before slicing.
8. Slice and Enjoy:
    - Slice the BBQ meatloaf into thick slices and serve hot, accompanied by your favorite side dishes such as mashed potatoes, roasted vegetables, or a crisp salad.

BBQ meatloaf is a delicious and satisfying dish that's perfect for a cozy family dinner or gathering with friends. The combination of savory meatloaf and tangy barbecue sauce is sure to please everyone's taste buds, making it a favorite comfort food classic.

Smoked Sausages with BBQ Sauce

Ingredients:

- 1 package of smoked sausages (such as kielbasa, bratwurst, or your favorite variety)
- 1 cup BBQ sauce (homemade or store-bought)
- 1 tablespoon olive oil (optional, for basting)

Instructions:

1. Preheat the Grill or Smoker:
    - Preheat your grill or smoker to medium-high heat, around 375-400°F (190-204°C). If using a smoker, set it up for indirect cooking.
2. Prepare the Sausages:
    - If the sausages are uncooked, you may want to parboil them first to ensure they are fully cooked through. Otherwise, you can use fully cooked smoked sausages straight from the package.
3. Grill or Smoke the Sausages:
    - Place the sausages on the grill or smoker grates, arranging them in a single layer.
    - Cook the sausages for 10-15 minutes, turning occasionally, until they are heated through and have nice grill marks or a smoky flavor.
4. Baste with BBQ Sauce (Optional):
    - If desired, you can baste the sausages with BBQ sauce during the last few minutes of cooking for extra flavor. Simply brush the sauce onto the sausages using a pastry brush or spoon.
5. Serve:
    - Once the sausages are cooked to your liking and heated through, remove them from the grill or smoker.
    - Serve the smoked sausages hot, with additional BBQ sauce on the side for dipping or drizzling.
6. Enjoy:
    - Enjoy the delicious flavor of smoked sausages with BBQ sauce as a main dish, appetizer, or addition to sandwiches, salads, or pasta dishes.
    - These smoked sausages are perfect for serving at cookouts, tailgates, or casual gatherings with family and friends.

Smoked sausages with BBQ sauce are a simple yet flavorful dish that's sure to be a hit with everyone. The smoky, savory sausages pair perfectly with the sweet and tangy BBQ sauce, creating a delicious combination that's hard to resist!

BBQ Pork Shoulder

Ingredients:

- 1 pork shoulder (4-6 pounds)
- Your favorite dry rub seasoning
- Wood chips or chunks for smoking (hickory, applewood, or cherry wood are great choices)
- BBQ sauce (optional, for serving)

Instructions:

1. Prepare the Pork Shoulder:
   - Rinse the pork shoulder under cold water and pat it dry with paper towels.
   - Trim any excess fat from the surface of the meat, leaving a thin layer for flavor and moisture.
2. Season the Pork Shoulder:
   - Season the pork shoulder generously with your favorite dry rub seasoning, covering all sides of the meat. You can use a store-bought rub or make your own blend of spices.
3. Preheat the Smoker:
   - Preheat your smoker to 225-250°F (107-121°C). Use wood chips or chunks for smoking; hickory, applewood, or cherry wood impart excellent flavor to pork shoulder.
4. Smoke the Pork Shoulder:
   - Place the seasoned pork shoulder on the smoker rack, fat side up, and close the lid.
   - Smoke the pork shoulder for approximately 1.5 to 2 hours per pound, or until it reaches an internal temperature of 195-205°F (91-96°C) and is tender and easily shredded with a fork.
5. Baste with BBQ Sauce (Optional):
   - If desired, you can baste the pork shoulder with BBQ sauce during the last hour of smoking, applying several coats and allowing each layer to caramelize slightly before adding the next.
6. Rest and Serve:
   - Once the pork shoulder is done smoking, remove it from the smoker and let it rest for 20-30 minutes before shredding.
   - Use two forks to shred the pork shoulder into bite-sized pieces, discarding any large pieces of fat or connective tissue.
7. Serve:

- Serve the shredded BBQ pork shoulder hot, with additional BBQ sauce on the side for dipping or drizzling.
- Enjoy the rich, smoky flavor and tender texture of this homemade BBQ pork shoulder with your favorite barbecue sides such as coleslaw, baked beans, or cornbread.

BBQ pork shoulder is a delicious and versatile dish that's perfect for feeding a crowd or enjoying leftovers throughout the week. Whether served as a sandwich filling, taco filling, or main dish, it's sure to be a hit with family and friends!

Kansas City Rib Tips

Ingredients:

- 2 pounds pork rib tips
- Your favorite dry rub seasoning
- BBQ sauce (homemade or store-bought)
- Wood chips or chunks for smoking (hickory, applewood, or cherry wood work well)

Instructions:

1. Prepare the Rib Tips:
   - Rinse the rib tips under cold water and pat them dry with paper towels.
   - Trim any excess fat from the rib tips, if desired.
2. Season the Rib Tips:
   - Season the rib tips generously with your favorite dry rub seasoning, covering all sides of the meat. You can use a store-bought rub or make your own blend of spices.
3. Preheat the Smoker:
   - Preheat your smoker to 225-250°F (107-121°C). Use wood chips or chunks for smoking; hickory, applewood, or cherry wood impart excellent flavor to rib tips.
4. Smoke the Rib Tips:
   - Place the seasoned rib tips on the smoker rack, bone side down, and close the lid.
   - Smoke the rib tips for approximately 2-3 hours, or until they are tender and the internal temperature reaches 190-200°F (88-93°C) when measured with a meat thermometer inserted into the thickest part of the meat.
5. Wrap (Optional):
   - If desired, you can wrap the rib tips in aluminum foil during the last hour of smoking to help retain moisture and tenderness.
6. Glaze with BBQ Sauce:
   - Once the rib tips are cooked through and tender, remove them from the smoker and brush them with BBQ sauce on all sides.
7. Finish Cooking:
   - Return the glazed rib tips to the smoker and cook for an additional 15-30 minutes, or until the BBQ sauce is caramelized and sticky.
8. Rest and Serve:

- Once the rib tips are done cooking, remove them from the smoker and let them rest for a few minutes before serving.

9. Serve:
    - Serve the Kansas City rib tips hot, with additional BBQ sauce on the side for dipping or drizzling.
    - Enjoy the rich, smoky flavor and tender texture of these delicious rib tips with your favorite barbecue sides.

Kansas City rib tips are a mouthwatering barbecue delicacy that's sure to be a hit at any cookout or gathering. With their savory flavor and juicy tenderness, they're a perfect choice for barbecue enthusiasts and meat lovers alike!

Smoked Beef Brisket Sandwiches

Ingredients:

- 1 whole beef brisket (about 8-10 pounds)
- Your favorite beef dry rub seasoning
- Wood chips or chunks for smoking (hickory, oak, or mesquite wood work well)
- 8-10 sandwich buns
- BBQ sauce (homemade or store-bought)
- Optional toppings: coleslaw, pickles, onions, cheese, lettuce, tomato

Instructions:

1. Prepare the Beef Brisket:
   - Trim any excess fat from the surface of the brisket, leaving a thin layer for flavor and moisture.
   - Season the brisket generously with your favorite beef dry rub seasoning, covering all sides of the meat. You can use a store-bought rub or make your own blend of spices.
2. Preheat the Smoker:
   - Preheat your smoker to 225-250°F (107-121°C). Use wood chips or chunks for smoking; hickory, oak, or mesquite wood impart excellent flavor to beef brisket.
3. Smoke the Brisket:
   - Place the seasoned brisket on the smoker rack, fat side up, and close the lid.
   - Smoke the brisket for approximately 1 hour per pound, or until it reaches an internal temperature of 195-205°F (91-96°C) when measured with a meat thermometer inserted into the thickest part of the meat.
4. Rest the Brisket:
   - Once the brisket is done smoking, remove it from the smoker and let it rest for at least 30 minutes, tented loosely with foil, to allow the juices to redistribute.
5. Slice the Brisket:
   - Use a sharp knife to slice the brisket thinly against the grain, ensuring tender and juicy slices.
6. Assemble the Sandwiches:
   - Toast the sandwich buns lightly if desired.
   - Place a generous portion of sliced brisket on the bottom half of each bun.

- Drizzle BBQ sauce over the brisket slices, and add any desired toppings such as coleslaw, pickles, onions, cheese, lettuce, or tomato.
7. Serve:
    - Top each sandwich with the remaining half of the bun and serve immediately.
    - Enjoy the smoky flavor and melt-in-your-mouth tenderness of these delicious smoked beef brisket sandwiches!

Smoked beef brisket sandwiches are a crowd-pleasing favorite that's perfect for any barbecue or casual gathering. Whether served as a main course or part of a buffet, they're sure to be a hit with family and friends!

BBQ Pulled Chicken

Ingredients:

- 2 pounds boneless, skinless chicken breasts or thighs
- 1 cup BBQ sauce (homemade or store-bought)
- 1/2 cup chicken broth or water
- 1 tablespoon olive oil
- 1 onion, finely chopped
- 2 cloves garlic, minced
- 1 teaspoon smoked paprika
- 1 teaspoon chili powder
- 1/2 teaspoon cumin
- Salt and pepper to taste
- Sandwich buns or rolls, for serving
- Optional toppings: coleslaw, pickles, onions, cheese, lettuce, tomato

Instructions:

1. Prepare the Chicken:
    - Season the chicken breasts or thighs with smoked paprika, chili powder, cumin, salt, and pepper.
2. Sear the Chicken:
    - Heat olive oil in a large skillet or Dutch oven over medium-high heat.
    - Add the seasoned chicken to the skillet and sear on both sides until golden brown, about 2-3 minutes per side. This step adds flavor and helps to seal in the juices.
3. Saute Onion and Garlic:
    - Add the chopped onion to the skillet and sauté for 2-3 minutes, until softened.
    - Add the minced garlic and sauté for an additional 1 minute, until fragrant.
4. Combine Ingredients:
    - Pour the chicken broth or water into the skillet, scraping up any browned bits from the bottom of the pan.
    - Stir in the BBQ sauce, coating the chicken and onions evenly.
5. Cook the Chicken:
    - Reduce the heat to low, cover the skillet, and let the chicken simmer gently for 20-25 minutes, or until cooked through and tender. If using chicken breasts, they may cook faster than thighs, so adjust the cooking time accordingly.

6. Shred the Chicken:
   - Once the chicken is cooked through, use two forks to shred it directly in the skillet. The chicken should be tender and easily pulled apart.
7. Simmer:
   - Continue to simmer the shredded chicken in the BBQ sauce for an additional 5-10 minutes, allowing the flavors to meld together and the sauce to thicken slightly.
8. Serve:
   - Serve the BBQ pulled chicken hot, piled high on sandwich buns or rolls.
   - Add optional toppings such as coleslaw, pickles, onions, cheese, lettuce, or tomato to customize each sandwich to your liking.
9. Enjoy:
   - Enjoy the delicious flavor and tender texture of this homemade BBQ pulled chicken as a satisfying and crowd-pleasing meal!

BBQ pulled chicken is a versatile dish that's perfect for feeding a crowd or enjoying as a quick and easy meal at home. With its sweet, tangy, and smoky flavor, it's sure to become a family favorite!

BBQ Stuffed Jalapeños

Ingredients:

- 12-15 large jalapeño peppers
- 8 ounces cream cheese, softened
- 1/2 cup shredded cheddar cheese
- 1/4 cup BBQ sauce (homemade or store-bought)
- 1/4 cup cooked and crumbled bacon (optional)
- 1/4 cup chopped green onions (optional)
- Salt and pepper to taste
- Toothpicks, for securing

Instructions:

1. Prepare the Jalapeños:
    - Cut the jalapeños in half lengthwise and remove the seeds and membranes using a small spoon or knife. Wear gloves to protect your hands from the spicy oils.
2. Make the Filling:
    - In a mixing bowl, combine the softened cream cheese, shredded cheddar cheese, BBQ sauce, cooked and crumbled bacon (if using), chopped green onions (if using), salt, and pepper. Mix until well combined.
3. Fill the Jalapeños:
    - Spoon the cream cheese mixture into each jalapeño half, filling them generously. Press the filling down slightly to compact it.
4. Secure with Toothpicks:
    - If desired, you can secure each stuffed jalapeño half with a toothpick to help hold the filling in place during grilling or baking.
5. Grill or Bake:
    - Preheat your grill to medium heat or preheat your oven to 375°F (190°C).
    - Place the stuffed jalapeños on the grill grates or on a baking sheet lined with parchment paper.
    - Grill or bake the stuffed jalapeños for 10-15 minutes, or until the peppers are tender and the filling is hot and bubbly.
6. Serve:
    - Once the stuffed jalapeños are cooked through, remove them from the grill or oven.
    - Serve the BBQ stuffed jalapeños hot as a delicious appetizer or snack.
7. Enjoy:

- Enjoy the spicy kick and creamy texture of these BBQ stuffed jalapeños with family and friends!

BBQ stuffed jalapeños are sure to be a hit at any gathering, and you can easily adjust the level of spiciness by removing more or fewer seeds and membranes from the jalapeños. Customize the filling with your favorite ingredients for a tasty twist on this classic appetizer!

BBQ Mac and Cheese

Ingredients:

- 12 ounces elbow macaroni (or your favorite pasta shape)
- 4 tablespoons unsalted butter
- 1/4 cup all-purpose flour
- 2 cups milk
- 2 cups shredded cheddar cheese
- 1 cup shredded mozzarella cheese
- 1/2 cup grated Parmesan cheese
- 1/2 cup BBQ sauce (homemade or store-bought)
- Salt and pepper to taste
- Optional toppings: crumbled bacon, chopped green onions, diced tomatoes

Instructions:

1. Cook the Pasta:
    - Cook the elbow macaroni according to the package instructions in a large pot of salted boiling water until al dente. Drain and set aside.
2. Make the Cheese Sauce:
    - In the same pot, melt the butter over medium heat. Once melted, whisk in the flour to create a roux, and cook for 1-2 minutes until lightly golden brown.
    - Gradually whisk in the milk, stirring constantly to prevent lumps from forming. Cook until the sauce thickens and coats the back of a spoon, about 5-7 minutes.
    - Reduce the heat to low and gradually stir in the shredded cheddar, mozzarella, and Parmesan cheeses until melted and smooth. Season with salt and pepper to taste.
3. Combine with BBQ Sauce:
    - Remove the cheese sauce from the heat and stir in the BBQ sauce until well combined. Taste and adjust seasoning if needed.
4. Combine with Pasta:
    - Add the cooked macaroni to the cheese sauce and stir until the pasta is evenly coated with the sauce.
5. Optional Toppings:
    - If desired, sprinkle the top of the mac and cheese with crumbled bacon, chopped green onions, diced tomatoes, or any other toppings of your choice.

6. Bake:
    - Preheat your oven to 350°F (175°C). Transfer the BBQ mac and cheese to a baking dish or cast-iron skillet.
7. Bake the Mac and Cheese:
    - Bake the mac and cheese in the preheated oven for 20-25 minutes, or until bubbly and golden brown on top.
8. Serve:
    - Once baked, remove the BBQ mac and cheese from the oven and let it cool for a few minutes before serving.
    - Serve the BBQ mac and cheese hot as a delicious and comforting main dish or side dish.
9. Enjoy:
    - Enjoy the creamy, cheesy goodness and smoky flavor of this homemade BBQ mac and cheese with family and friends!

BBQ mac and cheese is a crowd-pleasing favorite that's perfect for potlucks, cookouts, or any occasion where you want to serve up a hearty and comforting dish. Feel free to customize the recipe with your favorite cheeses, BBQ sauce, and toppings for a unique twist!

Smoked Pork Chops

Ingredients:

- 4 pork chops, bone-in or boneless (about 1 inch thick)
- Your favorite pork dry rub seasoning
- Wood chips or chunks for smoking (applewood, hickory, or cherry wood work well)
- Olive oil or melted butter for basting (optional)

Instructions:

1. Prepare the Pork Chops:
    - Rinse the pork chops under cold water and pat them dry with paper towels.
    - Trim any excess fat from the edges of the pork chops, if desired.
2. Season the Pork Chops:
    - Season the pork chops generously with your favorite pork dry rub seasoning, covering all sides of the meat. You can use a store-bought rub or make your own blend of spices.
3. Preheat the Smoker:
    - Preheat your smoker to 225-250°F (107-121°C). Use wood chips or chunks for smoking; applewood, hickory, or cherry wood impart excellent flavor to pork chops.
4. Smoke the Pork Chops:
    - Place the seasoned pork chops on the smoker rack, leaving some space between each chop for the smoke to circulate.
    - Close the lid and let the pork chops smoke for approximately 1-1.5 hours, or until they reach an internal temperature of 145°F (63°C) when measured with a meat thermometer inserted into the thickest part of the chop.
5. Baste with Olive Oil or Butter (Optional):
    - If desired, you can baste the pork chops with olive oil or melted butter during the last 30 minutes of smoking to help keep them moist and enhance their flavor.
6. Rest and Serve:
    - Once the pork chops are done smoking, remove them from the smoker and let them rest for 5-10 minutes before serving.
7. Serve:
    - Serve the smoked pork chops hot as a delicious and flavorful main dish.
8. Enjoy:

- Enjoy the smoky flavor and juicy tenderness of these homemade smoked pork chops with your favorite sides such as mashed potatoes, roasted vegetables, or a crisp salad!

Smoked pork chops are a delicious and easy-to-make dish that's perfect for any occasion. Whether served for a weeknight dinner or a weekend barbecue, they're sure to be a hit with family and friends!

BBQ Potato Salad

Ingredients:

- 2 pounds potatoes (Yukon Gold or Russet), peeled and diced
- 4 slices bacon, cooked and crumbled
- 1/2 cup mayonnaise
- 1/4 cup BBQ sauce (homemade or store-bought)
- 2 tablespoons apple cider vinegar
- 1 tablespoon Dijon mustard
- 1/2 cup diced red onion
- 1/4 cup diced celery
- 1/4 cup diced red bell pepper
- 2 tablespoons chopped fresh parsley
- Salt and pepper to taste
- Optional garnish: additional chopped parsley, sliced green onions

Instructions:

1. Cook the Potatoes:
    - Place the diced potatoes in a large pot and cover them with water. Add a pinch of salt to the water.
    - Bring the water to a boil over medium-high heat, then reduce the heat to medium-low and simmer the potatoes for 10-15 minutes, or until tender when pierced with a fork.
    - Drain the cooked potatoes and rinse them under cold water to cool them down. Transfer the potatoes to a large mixing bowl.
2. Prepare the Dressing:
    - In a small bowl, whisk together the mayonnaise, BBQ sauce, apple cider vinegar, and Dijon mustard until smooth and well combined. Adjust the amount of BBQ sauce to taste.
3. Assemble the Salad:
    - Add the crumbled bacon, diced red onion, diced celery, diced red bell pepper, and chopped parsley to the bowl with the cooked potatoes.
    - Pour the BBQ dressing over the potato mixture and gently toss until everything is evenly coated.
4. Season to Taste:
    - Taste the potato salad and season with salt and pepper to taste. Adjust the seasoning as needed.
5. Chill and Serve:

- Cover the BBQ potato salad and refrigerate it for at least 1 hour to allow the flavors to meld together.
- Before serving, garnish the potato salad with additional chopped parsley and sliced green onions, if desired.

6. Enjoy:
    - Serve the BBQ potato salad cold as a delicious side dish or accompaniment to grilled meats, burgers, or sandwiches.
    - Enjoy the smoky BBQ flavor and creamy texture of this homemade BBQ potato salad with family and friends!

BBQ potato salad is a tasty and satisfying dish that's perfect for picnics, potlucks, or any summer gathering. With its flavorful combination of tender potatoes, smoky bacon, crunchy vegetables, and tangy BBQ dressing, it's sure to be a hit with everyone!

Kansas City-style Burnt Ends Chili

Ingredients:

- 1 pound Kansas City-style burnt ends, chopped into bite-sized pieces
- 1 onion, diced
- 2 cloves garlic, minced
- 1 bell pepper, diced
- 1 can (14.5 ounces) diced tomatoes
- 1 can (15 ounces) kidney beans, drained and rinsed
- 1 can (15 ounces) black beans, drained and rinsed
- 1 cup beef broth
- 1/4 cup tomato paste
- 2 tablespoons chili powder
- 1 teaspoon ground cumin
- 1 teaspoon smoked paprika
- Salt and pepper to taste
- Optional toppings: shredded cheese, sour cream, sliced green onions, diced avocado, chopped cilantro

Instructions:

1. Sauté the Vegetables:
    - Heat a large pot or Dutch oven over medium heat. Add a splash of oil and sauté the diced onion, minced garlic, and diced bell pepper until softened, about 5-7 minutes.
2. Add Burnt Ends:
    - Add the chopped burnt ends to the pot and cook for an additional 5 minutes, stirring occasionally, to brown the meat slightly and develop flavor.
3. Combine Ingredients:
    - Stir in the diced tomatoes, kidney beans, black beans, beef broth, tomato paste, chili powder, ground cumin, smoked paprika, salt, and pepper. Mix until well combined.
4. Simmer:
    - Bring the chili to a simmer, then reduce the heat to low and cover the pot. Let the chili simmer gently for 30-40 minutes, stirring occasionally, to allow the flavors to meld together and the chili to thicken.
5. Adjust Seasoning:

- Taste the chili and adjust the seasoning as needed, adding more chili powder, cumin, smoked paprika, salt, or pepper to suit your taste preferences.
6. Serve:
    - Ladle the Kansas City-style burnt ends chili into bowls and garnish with your favorite toppings such as shredded cheese, sour cream, sliced green onions, diced avocado, or chopped cilantro.
7. Enjoy:
    - Serve the chili hot and enjoy the rich, smoky flavor and hearty texture of this delicious Kansas City-style burnt ends chili!

This Kansas City-style burnt ends chili is perfect for warming up on a chilly day or serving at a casual gathering with family and friends. With its bold flavors and tender chunks of burnt ends, it's sure to be a crowd-pleaser!

Smoked Beef Short Ribs

Ingredients:

- 4 beef short ribs, bone-in (about 2-3 pounds)
- Your favorite beef dry rub seasoning
- Wood chips or chunks for smoking (hickory, oak, or pecan wood work well)
- BBQ sauce (optional, for serving)

Instructions:

1. Prepare the Beef Short Ribs:
    - Trim any excess fat from the surface of the beef short ribs, leaving a thin layer for flavor and moisture.
    - Season the beef short ribs generously with your favorite beef dry rub seasoning, covering all sides of the meat. You can use a store-bought rub or make your own blend of spices.
2. Preheat the Smoker:
    - Preheat your smoker to 225-250°F (107-121°C). Use wood chips or chunks for smoking; hickory, oak, or pecan wood impart excellent flavor to beef short ribs.
3. Smoke the Beef Short Ribs:
    - Place the seasoned beef short ribs on the smoker rack, bone-side down, and close the lid.
    - Smoke the beef short ribs for approximately 5-6 hours, or until they reach an internal temperature of 195-205°F (91-96°C) when measured with a meat thermometer inserted into the thickest part of the meat.
4. Wrap in Foil (Optional):
    - If desired, you can wrap the beef short ribs in aluminum foil during the last hour of smoking to help retain moisture and tenderness.
5. Rest the Beef Short Ribs:
    - Once the beef short ribs are done smoking, remove them from the smoker and let them rest for 20-30 minutes before serving. This allows the juices to redistribute and the meat to become even more tender.
6. Serve:
    - Serve the smoked beef short ribs hot, with BBQ sauce on the side for dipping or drizzling if desired.
7. Enjoy:
    - Enjoy the rich, smoky flavor and tender texture of these delicious smoked beef short ribs as a main dish or as part of a barbecue feast!

Smoked beef short ribs are a classic barbecue favorite that's sure to impress with their savory flavor and fall-off-the-bone tenderness. Whether served at a backyard cookout or special occasion, they're sure to be a hit with family and friends!

BBQ Coleslaw

Ingredients:

- 1 small head of green cabbage, finely shredded
- 1 large carrot, grated
- 1/2 cup mayonnaise
- 2 tablespoons BBQ sauce (homemade or store-bought)
- 1 tablespoon apple cider vinegar
- 1 teaspoon Dijon mustard
- 1 teaspoon honey (optional, for sweetness)
- Salt and pepper to taste
- Optional add-ins: diced red onion, chopped cilantro, sliced green onions

Instructions:

1. Prepare the Vegetables:
    - Finely shred the green cabbage using a sharp knife or a mandoline slicer.
    - Grate the carrot using a box grater or a food processor fitted with a grating attachment.
    - Place the shredded cabbage and grated carrot in a large mixing bowl.
2. Make the Dressing:
    - In a small bowl, whisk together the mayonnaise, BBQ sauce, apple cider vinegar, Dijon mustard, honey (if using), salt, and pepper until smooth and well combined. Adjust the amount of BBQ sauce to taste.
3. Combine Ingredients:
    - Pour the BBQ dressing over the shredded cabbage and grated carrot in the mixing bowl.
    - Toss the coleslaw until the vegetables are evenly coated with the dressing.
4. Add Optional Add-Ins:
    - If desired, add diced red onion, chopped cilantro, or sliced green onions to the coleslaw for extra flavor and texture. Mix until well combined.
5. Chill and Serve:
    - Cover the BBQ coleslaw and refrigerate it for at least 1 hour to allow the flavors to meld together and the coleslaw to chill.
6. Stir Before Serving:
    - Before serving, give the BBQ coleslaw a good stir to redistribute the dressing and ensure that all the vegetables are coated.
7. Enjoy:

- Serve the BBQ coleslaw cold as a delicious side dish or accompaniment to grilled meats, sandwiches, or barbecue fare.
- Enjoy the tangy, smoky flavor and crunchy texture of this homemade BBQ coleslaw with family and friends!

BBQ coleslaw is a refreshing and flavorful side dish that's perfect for picnics, barbecues, or any summer gathering. With its zesty dressing and crisp vegetables, it's sure to be a hit with everyone! Feel free to adjust the ingredients and seasonings to suit your taste preferences.

BBQ Chicken Skewers

Ingredients:

- 1 pound boneless, skinless chicken breasts or thighs, cut into 1-inch cubes
- 1/2 cup BBQ sauce (homemade or store-bought)
- 2 tablespoons olive oil
- 1 tablespoon honey (optional, for sweetness)
- 1 tablespoon soy sauce
- 1 teaspoon smoked paprika
- 1/2 teaspoon garlic powder
- Salt and pepper to taste
- Wooden or metal skewers

Instructions:

1. Prepare the Chicken:
   - If using wooden skewers, soak them in water for at least 30 minutes to prevent them from burning on the grill.
   - Cut the chicken breasts or thighs into 1-inch cubes and set aside.
2. Make the BBQ Marinade:
   - In a small bowl, whisk together the BBQ sauce, olive oil, honey (if using), soy sauce, smoked paprika, garlic powder, salt, and pepper until well combined.
3. Marinate the Chicken:
   - Place the chicken cubes in a shallow dish or resealable plastic bag.
   - Pour the BBQ marinade over the chicken, making sure each piece is coated evenly. Marinate the chicken in the refrigerator for at least 30 minutes, or up to 4 hours for maximum flavor.
4. Preheat the Grill or Grill Pan:
   - Preheat your grill to medium-high heat, or heat a grill pan over medium-high heat on the stovetop.
5. Assemble the Skewers:
   - Thread the marinated chicken cubes onto the skewers, leaving a small space between each piece to ensure even cooking.
6. Grill the Skewers:
   - Place the chicken skewers on the preheated grill or grill pan.
   - Cook the skewers for 6-8 minutes per side, or until the chicken is cooked through and has grill marks on all sides. Baste the skewers with any remaining marinade during cooking for extra flavor.

7. Check for Doneness:
    - Use a meat thermometer to ensure the internal temperature of the chicken reaches 165°F (74°C) before removing it from the grill.
8. Serve:
    - Once the BBQ chicken skewers are cooked through, remove them from the grill and let them rest for a few minutes.
    - Serve the skewers hot as a delicious and flavorful main dish or appetizer.
9. Enjoy:
    - Enjoy the juicy, tender, and smoky flavor of these homemade BBQ chicken skewers with your favorite sides such as rice, salad, or grilled vegetables!

BBQ chicken skewers are a crowd-pleasing favorite that's perfect for summer cookouts, potlucks, or any occasion where you want to serve up a delicious and easy-to-make dish. Customize the recipe with your favorite BBQ sauce and seasonings for a personalized touch!

Smoked Pork Loin

Ingredients:

- 1 pork loin roast (about 3-4 pounds)
- Your favorite pork dry rub seasoning
- Wood chips or chunks for smoking (applewood, hickory, or cherry wood work well)
- Olive oil or mustard (optional, for binding)

Instructions:

1. Prepare the Pork Loin:
    - If desired, trim any excess fat from the surface of the pork loin roast, leaving a thin layer for flavor and moisture.
    - Pat the pork loin dry with paper towels.
2. Season the Pork Loin:
    - Season the pork loin generously with your favorite pork dry rub seasoning, covering all sides of the meat. You can use a store-bought rub or make your own blend of spices.
    - Optionally, you can brush the surface of the pork loin with olive oil or mustard before applying the dry rub. This helps the rub adhere to the meat and creates a flavorful crust during smoking.
3. Preheat the Smoker:
    - Preheat your smoker to 225-250°F (107-121°C). Use wood chips or chunks for smoking; applewood, hickory, or cherry wood impart excellent flavor to pork loin.
4. Smoke the Pork Loin:
    - Place the seasoned pork loin directly on the smoker rack, fat side up, and close the lid.
    - Smoke the pork loin for approximately 2-3 hours, or until it reaches an internal temperature of 145°F (63°C) when measured with a meat thermometer inserted into the thickest part of the meat.
5. Rest the Pork Loin:
    - Once the pork loin is done smoking, remove it from the smoker and let it rest for 10-15 minutes before slicing. This allows the juices to redistribute and the meat to become even more tender.
6. Slice and Serve:
    - Use a sharp knife to slice the smoked pork loin into thin slices.
    - Serve the smoked pork loin hot as a delicious and flavorful main dish.

7. Enjoy:
    - Enjoy the smoky flavor and juicy tenderness of this homemade smoked pork loin with your favorite sides such as roasted vegetables, mashed potatoes, or a crisp salad!

Smoked pork loin is a versatile dish that's perfect for feeding a crowd or enjoying as a special meal at home. With its rich flavor and tender texture, it's sure to be a hit with family and friends!

BBQ Beef Brisket Burnt Ends

Ingredients:

For the Brisket:

- 1 whole beef brisket (approximately 10-12 pounds)
- Your favorite beef dry rub seasoning
- Wood chips or chunks for smoking (hickory, oak, or pecan wood work well)

For the BBQ Sauce Glaze:

- 1 cup BBQ sauce (homemade or store-bought)
- 1/4 cup honey
- 2 tablespoons apple cider vinegar
- 1 tablespoon Worcestershire sauce
- 1 teaspoon smoked paprika
- Salt and pepper to taste

Instructions:

Smoking the Brisket:

1. Prepare the Brisket:
    - Trim excess fat from the surface of the brisket, leaving a thin layer for flavor and moisture.
    - Season the brisket generously with your favorite beef dry rub seasoning, covering all sides of the meat. You can use a store-bought rub or make your own blend of spices.
2. Preheat the Smoker:
    - Preheat your smoker to 225-250°F (107-121°C). Use wood chips or chunks for smoking; hickory, oak, or pecan wood impart excellent flavor to brisket.
3. Smoke the Brisket:
    - Place the seasoned brisket on the smoker rack, fat side up, and close the lid.
    - Smoke the brisket for approximately 1 hour per pound, or until it reaches an internal temperature of 195-205°F (91-96°C) when measured with a meat thermometer inserted into the thickest part of the meat.
4. Rest the Brisket:

- Once the brisket is done smoking, remove it from the smoker and let it rest for at least 30 minutes before proceeding. This allows the juices to redistribute and the meat to become even more tender.

Making the Burnt Ends:

1. Slice the Brisket:
    - Use a sharp knife to slice the smoked brisket into 1-inch cubes, trimming off any excess fat if necessary.
2. Prepare the BBQ Sauce Glaze:
    - In a small saucepan, combine the BBQ sauce, honey, apple cider vinegar, Worcestershire sauce, smoked paprika, salt, and pepper. Heat the mixture over medium heat, stirring occasionally, until it comes to a simmer. Remove from heat.
3. Coat the Brisket Cubes:
    - Place the brisket cubes in a large mixing bowl and pour the BBQ sauce glaze over them. Toss the brisket cubes until they are evenly coated with the glaze.
4. Return to the Smoker:
    - Return the glazed brisket cubes to the smoker, placing them in a disposable aluminum foil pan or directly on the smoker rack.
5. Smoke Again:
    - Smoke the brisket cubes for an additional 1-2 hours, or until they are caramelized and tender, with a slightly crispy exterior.
6. Serve and Enjoy:
    - Remove the BBQ beef brisket burnt ends from the smoker and let them cool for a few minutes before serving.
    - Serve the burnt ends hot as a mouthwatering and irresistible appetizer, snack, or main dish.

BBQ beef brisket burnt ends are a true delicacy that's worth the time and effort. With their rich flavor and irresistible texture, they're sure to be a hit at your next barbecue or gathering!

Smoked Chicken Thighs

Ingredients:

- 6-8 bone-in, skin-on chicken thighs
- Your favorite poultry dry rub seasoning
- Wood chips or chunks for smoking (hickory, applewood, or cherry wood work well)
- Olive oil or melted butter (optional, for basting)

Instructions:

1. Prepare the Chicken Thighs:
    - Rinse the chicken thighs under cold water and pat them dry with paper towels.
    - Trim any excess skin or fat from the thighs, if desired.
2. Season the Chicken Thighs:
    - Season the chicken thighs generously with your favorite poultry dry rub seasoning, covering all sides of the meat. You can use a store-bought rub or make your own blend of spices.
3. Preheat the Smoker:
    - Preheat your smoker to 225-250°F (107-121°C). Use wood chips or chunks for smoking; hickory, applewood, or cherry wood impart excellent flavor to chicken thighs.
4. Smoke the Chicken Thighs:
    - Place the seasoned chicken thighs directly on the smoker rack, skin side up, leaving some space between each piece for smoke circulation.
    - Close the lid and let the chicken thighs smoke for approximately 2-2.5 hours, or until they reach an internal temperature of 165°F (74°C) when measured with a meat thermometer inserted into the thickest part of the meat.
5. Optional Basting:
    - If desired, you can baste the chicken thighs with olive oil or melted butter during the last 30 minutes of smoking to help keep them moist and enhance their flavor.
6. Check for Doneness:
    - Once the chicken thighs are cooked through and have reached the desired internal temperature, remove them from the smoker.
7. Rest and Serve:

- Let the smoked chicken thighs rest for a few minutes before serving to allow the juices to redistribute.
- Serve the smoked chicken thighs hot as a delicious and flavorful main dish.

8. Enjoy:
   - Enjoy the tender, juicy, and smoky flavor of these homemade smoked chicken thighs with your favorite sides such as coleslaw, cornbread, or grilled vegetables!

Smoked chicken thighs are a versatile dish that's perfect for any occasion. Whether served at a backyard barbecue, picnic, or family dinner, they're sure to be a hit with everyone! Feel free to customize the recipe with your favorite seasonings and sauces for a unique twist.

BBQ Pulled Pork Nachos

Ingredients:

- 1 pound cooked BBQ pulled pork
- 1 bag (about 10-12 ounces) tortilla chips
- 2 cups shredded cheese (cheddar, Monterey Jack, or a blend)
- 1/2 cup BBQ sauce (homemade or store-bought)
- 1/4 cup diced red onion
- 1/4 cup diced jalapeños (optional)
- 1/4 cup diced tomatoes
- 1/4 cup sliced black olives
- 1/4 cup chopped fresh cilantro
- Sour cream, guacamole, salsa, or other toppings of your choice

Instructions:

1. Preheat the Oven:
    - Preheat your oven to 375°F (190°C). Line a large baking sheet with parchment paper or aluminum foil for easy cleanup.
2. Assemble the Nachos:
    - Spread a single layer of tortilla chips evenly on the prepared baking sheet.
    - Sprinkle half of the shredded cheese over the tortilla chips.
    - Spread the cooked BBQ pulled pork evenly over the cheese layer.
    - Drizzle the BBQ sauce over the pulled pork.
3. Add Toppings:
    - Sprinkle the diced red onion, diced jalapeños (if using), diced tomatoes, and sliced black olives over the BBQ pulled pork layer.
    - Sprinkle the remaining shredded cheese evenly over the toppings.
4. Bake the Nachos:
    - Place the baking sheet in the preheated oven and bake for 10-12 minutes, or until the cheese is melted and bubbly, and the nachos are heated through.
5. Garnish and Serve:
    - Remove the nachos from the oven and sprinkle the chopped fresh cilantro over the top.
    - Serve the BBQ pulled pork nachos hot, straight from the baking sheet.
6. Add Additional Toppings (Optional):
    - Serve the nachos with additional toppings such as sour cream, guacamole, salsa, or any other toppings of your choice on the side.

7. Enjoy:
    - Dig into the delicious layers of BBQ pulled pork, melted cheese, and crunchy tortilla chips, and enjoy the flavor explosion of these homemade BBQ pulled pork nachos!

BBQ pulled pork nachos are perfect for game day gatherings, parties, or casual get-togethers with friends and family. Customize the toppings to suit your taste preferences and enjoy this irresistible and satisfying snack!

Kansas City BBQ Baked Potato

Ingredients:

- 4 large baking potatoes (such as Russet or Idaho)
- Olive oil
- Salt and pepper, to taste
- 1 cup cooked and shredded BBQ beef, pork, or chicken
- 1/2 cup shredded cheese (cheddar, Monterey Jack, or a blend)
- 1/4 cup diced red onion
- 1/4 cup diced green onions
- 1/4 cup diced tomatoes
- 1/4 cup sliced black olives
- 1/4 cup chopped fresh cilantro
- BBQ sauce (homemade or store-bought), for drizzling
- Sour cream, for serving (optional)

Instructions:

1. Preheat the Oven:
   - Preheat your oven to 400°F (200°C).
2. Prepare the Potatoes:
   - Scrub the potatoes clean under cold water and pat them dry with a paper towel.
   - Prick each potato several times with a fork to allow steam to escape during baking.
   - Rub the potatoes with olive oil and season generously with salt and pepper.
3. Bake the Potatoes:
   - Place the seasoned potatoes directly on the oven rack or on a baking sheet lined with aluminum foil.
   - Bake the potatoes for 45-60 minutes, or until they are tender when pierced with a fork.
4. Prepare the Toppings:
   - While the potatoes are baking, prepare the toppings. Cook and shred the BBQ beef, pork, or chicken if not already cooked.
   - Dice the red onion, green onions, tomatoes, and olives. Chop the fresh cilantro.
5. Assemble the BBQ Baked Potatoes:

- Once the potatoes are baked, carefully slice them open lengthwise using a knife.
- Fluff the insides of the potatoes with a fork.
- Divide the shredded BBQ meat evenly among the potatoes, placing it in the center of each potato.
- Sprinkle the shredded cheese over the BBQ meat.
- Top each potato with diced red onion, green onions, tomatoes, black olives, and chopped cilantro.

6. Serve:
    - Drizzle each BBQ baked potato with BBQ sauce, to taste.
    - Serve the BBQ baked potatoes hot, with sour cream on the side if desired.
7. Enjoy:
    - Dig into the delicious layers of fluffy baked potato, savory BBQ meat, melted cheese, and fresh toppings, and enjoy the flavor explosion of these Kansas City BBQ baked potatoes!

These BBQ baked potatoes make for a satisfying and comforting meal that's perfect for lunch or dinner. Customize the toppings to suit your taste preferences and enjoy this hearty dish with family and friends!

Smoked Beef Ribs

Ingredients:

- 3-4 pounds beef ribs (short ribs or plate ribs)
- Your favorite beef dry rub seasoning
- Wood chips or chunks for smoking (hickory, oak, or mesquite wood work well)

Instructions:

1. Prepare the Beef Ribs:
    - Rinse the beef ribs under cold water and pat them dry with paper towels.
    - Trim any excess fat from the surface of the ribs, leaving a thin layer for flavor and moisture.
2. Season the Beef Ribs:
    - Season the beef ribs generously with your favorite beef dry rub seasoning, covering all sides of the meat. You can use a store-bought rub or make your own blend of spices.
3. Preheat the Smoker:
    - Preheat your smoker to 225-250°F (107-121°C). Use wood chips or chunks for smoking; hickory, oak, or mesquite wood impart excellent flavor to beef ribs.
4. Smoke the Beef Ribs:
    - Place the seasoned beef ribs directly on the smoker rack, bone side down, leaving some space between each rib for smoke circulation.
    - Close the lid and let the beef ribs smoke for approximately 4-6 hours, or until they are tender and have reached an internal temperature of 195-205°F (91-96°C) when measured with a meat thermometer inserted into the thickest part of the meat.
5. Check for Doneness:
    - Once the beef ribs are cooked through and have reached the desired internal temperature, remove them from the smoker.
6. Rest and Serve:
    - Let the smoked beef ribs rest for 10-15 minutes before serving to allow the juices to redistribute.
    - Serve the smoked beef ribs hot as a delicious and satisfying main dish.
7. Enjoy:
    - Sink your teeth into the tender and flavorful meat of these homemade smoked beef ribs, and savor the rich, smoky flavor that's been infused into every bite!

Smoked beef ribs are a classic barbecue favorite that's perfect for serving at a backyard cookout, special occasion, or any time you're craving a hearty and flavorful dish. Enjoy these mouthwatering ribs with your favorite barbecue sides and sauces for a complete and satisfying meal!

BBQ Bacon-wrapped Shrimp

Ingredients:

- 1 pound large shrimp, peeled and deveined, tails left on
- 10-12 slices bacon, cut in half crosswise
- 1/2 cup BBQ sauce (homemade or store-bought)
- Wooden toothpicks or metal skewers

Instructions:

1. Preheat the Oven or Grill:
    - Preheat your oven to 400°F (200°C) or preheat your grill to medium-high heat.
2. Prepare the Shrimp:
    - Pat the shrimp dry with paper towels.
    - Season the shrimp with salt and pepper, to taste.
3. Wrap the Shrimp with Bacon:
    - Take each shrimp and wrap it with a half-slice of bacon, securing the bacon in place with a toothpick or skewer. Repeat with the remaining shrimp and bacon slices.
4. Brush with BBQ Sauce:
    - Brush each bacon-wrapped shrimp with BBQ sauce, coating it evenly on all sides.
5. Cook the Shrimp:
    - If using an oven, place the bacon-wrapped shrimp on a baking sheet lined with aluminum foil or a wire rack set over a baking sheet. Bake in the preheated oven for 10-15 minutes, or until the bacon is crispy and the shrimp are cooked through.
    - If using a grill, place the bacon-wrapped shrimp directly on the grill grates. Grill for 2-3 minutes per side, or until the bacon is crispy and the shrimp are cooked through.
6. Serve:
    - Once cooked, remove the BBQ bacon-wrapped shrimp from the oven or grill.
    - Serve the shrimp hot as a delicious appetizer or main dish.
7. Enjoy:
    - Enjoy the irresistible combination of smoky bacon, juicy shrimp, and tangy BBQ sauce in every bite of these BBQ bacon-wrapped shrimp!

BBQ bacon-wrapped shrimp is perfect for serving at parties, cookouts, or as a tasty appetizer before a barbecue feast. Serve them with additional BBQ sauce for dipping, if desired, and watch them disappear in no time!

BBQ Pulled Pork Pizza

Ingredients:

- 1 pre-made pizza crust or homemade pizza dough
- 1/2 cup BBQ sauce (homemade or store-bought)
- 1 cup cooked and shredded BBQ pulled pork
- 1 cup shredded mozzarella cheese
- 1/2 cup shredded cheddar cheese
- 1/4 cup thinly sliced red onion
- 1/4 cup sliced jalapeños (optional)
- Fresh cilantro leaves, for garnish (optional)

Instructions:

1. Preheat the Oven:
    - Preheat your oven to the temperature specified on the pizza crust or dough package (usually around 400-450°F or 200-230°C).
2. Prepare the Pizza Crust:
    - If using a pre-made pizza crust, follow the package instructions for pre-baking, if necessary.
    - If using homemade pizza dough, roll it out on a lightly floured surface into your desired shape and thickness.
3. Assemble the Pizza:
    - Spread the BBQ sauce evenly over the pizza crust, leaving a small border around the edges.
    - Sprinkle half of the shredded mozzarella cheese over the BBQ sauce.
    - Distribute the shredded BBQ pulled pork evenly over the cheese layer.
    - Sprinkle the remaining mozzarella cheese and shredded cheddar cheese over the pulled pork.
    - Scatter the thinly sliced red onion and sliced jalapeños (if using) over the cheese.
4. Bake the Pizza:
    - Place the assembled pizza on a baking sheet or pizza stone.
    - Bake in the preheated oven for 12-15 minutes, or until the cheese is melted and bubbly, and the crust is golden brown.
5. Garnish and Serve:
    - Once the pizza is baked, remove it from the oven.
    - Garnish with fresh cilantro leaves, if desired, for added flavor and freshness.

6. Slice and Enjoy:
    - Use a pizza cutter to slice the BBQ pulled pork pizza into wedges.
    - Serve hot and enjoy the delicious combination of flavors in every bite!

BBQ pulled pork pizza is perfect for a casual dinner, game day gathering, or any occasion when you're craving a tasty and satisfying meal. Customize the toppings to suit your taste preferences and enjoy this delicious homemade pizza with family and friends!

Smoked Turkey Legs

Ingredients:

- 4 turkey legs
- Your favorite poultry dry rub seasoning
- Wood chips or chunks for smoking (hickory, applewood, or cherry wood work well)

Instructions:

1. Prepare the Turkey Legs:
    - Rinse the turkey legs under cold water and pat them dry with paper towels.
    - Trim any excess skin or fat from the turkey legs, if desired.
2. Season the Turkey Legs:
    - Season the turkey legs generously with your favorite poultry dry rub seasoning, covering all sides of the meat. You can use a store-bought rub or make your own blend of spices.
3. Preheat the Smoker:
    - Preheat your smoker to 225-250°F (107-121°C). Use wood chips or chunks for smoking; hickory, applewood, or cherry wood impart excellent flavor to turkey legs.
4. Smoke the Turkey Legs:
    - Place the seasoned turkey legs directly on the smoker rack, bone side down, leaving some space between each leg for smoke circulation.
    - Close the lid and let the turkey legs smoke for approximately 3-4 hours, or until they reach an internal temperature of 165°F (74°C) when measured with a meat thermometer inserted into the thickest part of the meat.
5. Check for Doneness:
    - Once the turkey legs are cooked through and have reached the desired internal temperature, remove them from the smoker.
6. Rest and Serve:
    - Let the smoked turkey legs rest for a few minutes before serving to allow the juices to redistribute.
    - Serve the smoked turkey legs hot as a delicious and satisfying main dish.
7. Enjoy:
    - Sink your teeth into the tender and flavorful meat of these homemade smoked turkey legs, and savor the rich, smoky flavor that's been infused into every bite!

Smoked turkey legs are a favorite at festivals and outdoor events, but they're also easy to make at home. Enjoy these juicy and delicious turkey legs with your favorite sides for a memorable and satisfying meal!

Kansas City BBQ Beef Sandwiches

Ingredients:

- 2 pounds beef chuck roast or brisket
- 1 tablespoon olive oil
- Salt and pepper, to taste
- 1 cup beef broth
- 1 cup BBQ sauce (homemade or store-bought)
- 4-6 sandwich buns
- Optional toppings: sliced red onion, pickles, coleslaw

Instructions:

1. Preheat the Oven or Slow Cooker:
   - Preheat your oven to 325°F (163°C) or set your slow cooker to low heat.
2. Prepare the Beef:
   - Pat the beef chuck roast or brisket dry with paper towels.
   - Season the beef generously with salt and pepper on all sides.
3. Sear the Beef (Optional):
   - Heat the olive oil in a large skillet over medium-high heat.
   - Sear the beef on all sides until browned, about 3-4 minutes per side. This step adds extra flavor but can be skipped if you're short on time.
4. Cook the Beef:
   - Place the seared or unseared beef in a roasting pan or slow cooker.
   - Pour the beef broth over the beef.
   - Cover the roasting pan with aluminum foil or the slow cooker with its lid.
   - Cook the beef in the preheated oven for 3-4 hours or in the slow cooker for 6-8 hours, or until the beef is tender and easily shreds with a fork.
5. Shred the Beef:
   - Once the beef is cooked, transfer it to a cutting board and shred it using two forks or meat claws.
6. Add BBQ Sauce:
   - Place the shredded beef back into the roasting pan or slow cooker.
   - Pour the BBQ sauce over the shredded beef and stir to combine.
   - Cook for an additional 30 minutes in the oven or on low heat in the slow cooker to allow the flavors to meld.
7. Assemble the Sandwiches:
   - Split the sandwich buns and lightly toast them, if desired.
   - Place a generous amount of BBQ beef onto the bottom half of each bun.

- Top with optional toppings such as sliced red onion, pickles, or coleslaw, if desired.
- Place the top half of the bun on top of the BBQ beef.
8. Serve and Enjoy:
    - Serve the Kansas City BBQ beef sandwiches hot, with additional BBQ sauce on the side for dipping, if desired.
9. Enjoy:
    - Sink your teeth into the tender and flavorful BBQ beef sandwiches, and savor the rich, smoky flavor that's synonymous with Kansas City barbecue!

These Kansas City BBQ beef sandwiches are perfect for a weeknight dinner or a casual gathering with friends and family. Serve them with your favorite sides such as potato salad, coleslaw, or baked beans for a complete meal.

BBQ Stuffed Bell Peppers

Ingredients:

- 4 large bell peppers (any color), halved and seeds removed
- 1 pound ground beef or turkey
- 1 small onion, diced
- 2 cloves garlic, minced
- 1 cup cooked rice (white or brown)
- 1 cup BBQ sauce (homemade or store-bought), divided
- 1 cup shredded cheddar or Monterey Jack cheese
- Salt and pepper, to taste
- Optional toppings: chopped fresh cilantro, sliced green onions

Instructions:

1. Preheat the Oven:
    - Preheat your oven to 375°F (190°C).
2. Prepare the Bell Peppers:
    - Cut the bell peppers in half lengthwise and remove the seeds and membranes. Place the pepper halves in a baking dish, cut side up.
3. Prepare the Filling:
    - In a large skillet, cook the ground beef or turkey over medium heat until browned and cooked through, breaking it apart with a spoon as it cooks.
    - Add the diced onion and minced garlic to the skillet with the cooked meat. Cook for an additional 2-3 minutes, until the onion is soft and translucent.
    - Stir in the cooked rice and 1/2 cup of BBQ sauce. Season with salt and pepper, to taste. Cook for another 2-3 minutes to allow the flavors to meld.
4. Stuff the Bell Peppers:
    - Spoon the BBQ meat and rice mixture evenly into each bell pepper half, pressing down gently to pack the filling.
5. Top with Cheese and BBQ Sauce:
    - Sprinkle shredded cheese over the top of each stuffed bell pepper.
    - Drizzle the remaining 1/2 cup of BBQ sauce over the cheese.
6. Bake the Stuffed Bell Peppers:
    - Cover the baking dish with aluminum foil and bake in the preheated oven for 30-35 minutes, or until the bell peppers are tender and the filling is heated through.
7. Serve:

- Remove the stuffed bell peppers from the oven and let them cool for a few minutes before serving.
- Garnish with chopped fresh cilantro and sliced green onions, if desired.

8. Enjoy:
    - Serve the BBQ stuffed bell peppers hot as a delicious and satisfying main dish.

These BBQ stuffed bell peppers are a flavorful and nutritious meal that's sure to be a hit with family and friends. Customize the filling with your favorite ingredients and enjoy the sweet and savory flavors of these delicious stuffed peppers!

BBQ Chicken Pizza

Ingredients:

- 1 pre-made pizza crust or homemade pizza dough
- 1 cup cooked and shredded chicken breast or rotisserie chicken
- 1/2 cup BBQ sauce (homemade or store-bought)
- 1 cup shredded mozzarella cheese
- 1/2 cup shredded cheddar cheese
- 1/4 cup thinly sliced red onion
- 1/4 cup chopped fresh cilantro
- 2 tablespoons sliced green onions (optional)
- Olive oil, for brushing

Instructions:

1. Preheat the Oven:
    - Preheat your oven to the temperature specified on the pizza crust or dough package (usually around 400-450°F or 200-230°C).
2. Prepare the Pizza Crust:
    - If using a pre-made pizza crust, follow the package instructions for pre-baking, if necessary.
    - If using homemade pizza dough, roll it out on a lightly floured surface into your desired shape and thickness.
3. Assemble the Pizza:
    - Brush the edges of the pizza crust with olive oil for a golden crust.
    - Spread the BBQ sauce evenly over the pizza crust, leaving a small border around the edges.
    - Sprinkle half of the shredded mozzarella cheese over the BBQ sauce.
    - Distribute the shredded chicken evenly over the cheese layer.
    - Sprinkle the remaining mozzarella cheese and shredded cheddar cheese over the chicken.
    - Scatter the thinly sliced red onion over the cheese.
4. Bake the Pizza:
    - Place the assembled pizza on a baking sheet or pizza stone.
    - Bake in the preheated oven for 12-15 minutes, or until the cheese is melted and bubbly, and the crust is golden brown.
5. Garnish and Serve:
    - Once the pizza is baked, remove it from the oven.

- Sprinkle chopped fresh cilantro and sliced green onions (if using) over the top for added flavor and freshness.
6. Slice and Enjoy:
    - Use a pizza cutter to slice the BBQ chicken pizza into wedges.
    - Serve hot and enjoy the delicious combination of flavors in every bite!

BBQ chicken pizza is perfect for a weeknight dinner or a casual gathering with friends and family. Customize the toppings to suit your taste preferences and enjoy this delicious homemade pizza with your favorite sides!

Smoked Sausage and Pepper Skewers

Ingredients:

- 1 pound smoked sausage (such as kielbasa or Andouille), cut into 1-inch slices
- 2 bell peppers (any color), cut into 1-inch pieces
- 1 large red onion, cut into 1-inch pieces
- Wooden or metal skewers

Marinade (optional):

- 1/4 cup olive oil
- 2 tablespoons balsamic vinegar
- 2 cloves garlic, minced
- 1 teaspoon dried oregano
- 1 teaspoon dried thyme
- Salt and pepper, to taste

Instructions:

1. Preheat the Grill (if grilling):
    - Preheat your grill to medium-high heat.
2. Prepare the Skewers:
    - If using wooden skewers, soak them in water for at least 30 minutes to prevent them from burning on the grill.
    - Thread the smoked sausage slices, bell pepper pieces, and red onion pieces onto the skewers, alternating between the ingredients.
3. Prepare the Marinade (optional):
    - In a small bowl, whisk together the olive oil, balsamic vinegar, minced garlic, dried oregano, dried thyme, salt, and pepper to make the marinade.
4. Marinate the Skewers (optional):
    - If using the marinade, place the assembled skewers in a shallow dish or resealable plastic bag.
    - Pour the marinade over the skewers, making sure they are evenly coated.
    - Cover the dish or seal the bag and refrigerate for at least 30 minutes, or up to 4 hours, to allow the flavors to meld.
5. Grill the Skewers:
    - If grilling, place the skewers on the preheated grill.
    - Grill for 8-10 minutes, turning occasionally, until the sausage is heated through and the peppers and onions are tender and slightly charred.

6. Serve:
    - Once cooked, remove the skewers from the grill and transfer them to a serving platter.
    - Serve the smoked sausage and pepper skewers hot, with your favorite sides such as rice, potatoes, or a salad.
7. Enjoy:
    - Dig into the smoky, savory goodness of these delicious smoked sausage and pepper skewers, and enjoy the flavorful combination of sausage, peppers, and onions in every bite!

These smoked sausage and pepper skewers are perfect for a summer barbecue, tailgate party, or any occasion when you're craving a tasty and satisfying dish. Customize the ingredients and marinade to suit your taste preferences, and enjoy this easy and delicious recipe with family and friends!

BBQ Pulled Pork Tacos

Ingredients:

- 2 cups cooked and shredded BBQ pulled pork
- 8-10 small flour or corn tortillas
- 1 cup shredded lettuce or cabbage
- 1 cup diced tomatoes
- 1/2 cup diced red onion
- 1/4 cup chopped fresh cilantro
- 1/2 cup shredded cheese (cheddar, Monterey Jack, or a blend)
- BBQ sauce (homemade or store-bought)
- Lime wedges, for serving
- Optional toppings: sliced jalapeños, avocado slices, sour cream

Instructions:

1. Warm the Tortillas:
   - Heat the tortillas in a dry skillet over medium heat for about 30 seconds on each side, or until warmed through. Alternatively, you can wrap the tortillas in aluminum foil and warm them in a preheated oven at 350°F (175°C) for 5-10 minutes.
2. Assemble the Tacos:
   - Spoon a portion of the shredded BBQ pulled pork onto each warm tortilla.
   - Top the pulled pork with shredded lettuce or cabbage, diced tomatoes, diced red onion, chopped cilantro, and shredded cheese.
3. Drizzle with BBQ Sauce:
   - Drizzle each taco with BBQ sauce to taste. You can use your favorite homemade or store-bought BBQ sauce for this step.
4. Add Optional Toppings:
   - If desired, add additional toppings such as sliced jalapeños, avocado slices, or a dollop of sour cream to each taco.
5. Serve:
   - Serve the BBQ pulled pork tacos immediately, with lime wedges on the side for squeezing over the tacos.
6. Enjoy:
   - Enjoy the delicious combination of smoky pulled pork, tangy BBQ sauce, and fresh toppings in every bite of these BBQ pulled pork tacos!

BBQ pulled pork tacos are perfect for a casual dinner, game day gathering, or any occasion when you're craving a tasty and satisfying meal. Customize the toppings to suit your taste preferences and enjoy this flavorful twist on classic tacos with family and friends!

Kansas City BBQ Sliders

Ingredients:

- 1 pound cooked and shredded BBQ meat (pulled pork, shredded chicken, or beef brisket)
- 12 slider buns
- 1 cup BBQ sauce (homemade or store-bought)
- 1 cup coleslaw (homemade or store-bought)
- Pickles, for topping (optional)
- Slider bun toppings (optional): sliced red onion, lettuce, tomato slices

Instructions:

1. Warm the BBQ Meat:
    - Heat the shredded BBQ meat in a skillet or microwave until warmed through.
2. Toast the Slider Buns (optional):
    - If desired, lightly toast the slider buns in a toaster, oven, or skillet for added flavor and texture.
3. Assemble the Sliders:
    - Place a spoonful of warmed shredded BBQ meat on the bottom half of each slider bun.
    - Drizzle BBQ sauce over the meat on each slider.
    - Top with a spoonful of coleslaw.
    - Add any additional toppings such as pickles, sliced red onion, lettuce, or tomato slices, if desired.
4. Top with Bun:
    - Place the top half of each slider bun on top of the filling to complete the sliders.
5. Serve:
    - Arrange the Kansas City BBQ sliders on a platter and serve immediately.
6. Enjoy:
    - Enjoy the delicious combination of tender BBQ meat, tangy sauce, and crunchy coleslaw in every bite of these Kansas City BBQ sliders!

These sliders are perfect for serving at parties, picnics, or any casual gathering. They're easy to make and can be customized with your favorite BBQ meat and toppings. Serve them alongside chips, fries, or a fresh salad for a complete meal.

Smoked BBQ Meatballs

Ingredients:

For the Meatballs:

- 1 pound ground beef (or a mix of beef and pork)
- 1/2 cup breadcrumbs
- 1/4 cup grated Parmesan cheese
- 1/4 cup milk
- 1 egg
- 2 cloves garlic, minced
- 1 teaspoon onion powder
- 1 teaspoon dried oregano
- Salt and pepper, to taste

For the BBQ Sauce:

- 1 cup ketchup
- 1/4 cup brown sugar
- 2 tablespoons apple cider vinegar
- 1 tablespoon Worcestershire sauce
- 1 teaspoon smoked paprika
- 1/2 teaspoon garlic powder
- Salt and pepper, to taste

Instructions:

1. Preheat the Smoker:
    - Preheat your smoker to 225°F (107°C) using your choice of wood chips or chunks for smoking. Hickory, oak, or cherry wood work well with meatballs.
2. Make the Meatballs:
    - In a large bowl, combine the ground beef, breadcrumbs, grated Parmesan cheese, milk, egg, minced garlic, onion powder, dried oregano, salt, and pepper. Mix until well combined.
    - Shape the mixture into small meatballs, about 1 inch in diameter.
3. Smoke the Meatballs:
    - Place the meatballs on a smoker rack or a baking sheet lined with aluminum foil.

- Place the rack or baking sheet in the preheated smoker and smoke the meatballs for 1 to 1.5 hours, or until they are cooked through and have reached an internal temperature of 160°F (71°C).
4. Make the BBQ Sauce:
    - While the meatballs are smoking, prepare the BBQ sauce. In a small saucepan, combine the ketchup, brown sugar, apple cider vinegar, Worcestershire sauce, smoked paprika, garlic powder, salt, and pepper. Cook over medium heat, stirring occasionally, until the sauce is heated through and the sugar has dissolved. Remove from heat.
5. Glaze the Meatballs:
    - Once the meatballs are cooked, remove them from the smoker.
    - Brush the smoked meatballs with the prepared BBQ sauce, coating them evenly.
6. Serve:
    - Transfer the smoked BBQ meatballs to a serving platter.
    - Serve hot as appetizers or as a main course, garnished with chopped fresh parsley or green onions, if desired.
7. Enjoy:
    - Enjoy the smoky flavor and tender texture of these delicious smoked BBQ meatballs!

These smoked BBQ meatballs are sure to be a hit at any gathering. They're easy to make and packed with flavor, making them a crowd-pleasing dish for any occasion. Serve them with extra BBQ sauce on the side for dipping, if desired.

BBQ Chicken Drumsticks

Ingredients:

- 8 chicken drumsticks
- Salt and pepper, to taste
- 1 cup BBQ sauce (homemade or store-bought)
- 2 tablespoons olive oil
- Optional: BBQ rub or seasoning blend

Instructions:

1. Prepare the Chicken Drumsticks:
    - Pat the chicken drumsticks dry with paper towels.
    - Season the drumsticks generously with salt and pepper. Optionally, you can rub them with your favorite BBQ rub or seasoning blend for extra flavor.
2. Preheat the Grill or Oven:
    - If grilling, preheat your grill to medium-high heat (about 375-400°F or 190-200°C).
    - If baking, preheat your oven to 400°F (200°C).
3. Grill or Bake the Chicken Drumsticks:
    - If grilling: Brush the grill grates with oil to prevent sticking. Place the seasoned chicken drumsticks on the grill and cook for about 25-30 minutes, turning occasionally, until the chicken is cooked through and reaches an internal temperature of 165°F (74°C).
    - If baking: Place the seasoned chicken drumsticks on a baking sheet lined with aluminum foil or parchment paper. Bake in the preheated oven for 35-40 minutes, or until the chicken is cooked through and reaches an internal temperature of 165°F (74°C).
4. Apply BBQ Sauce:
    - In the last 10 minutes of cooking, brush the chicken drumsticks with BBQ sauce, turning them occasionally and brushing with more sauce, until the sauce caramelizes and forms a sticky glaze.
5. Serve:
    - Once cooked through and glazed with BBQ sauce, remove the chicken drumsticks from the grill or oven.
    - Let them rest for a few minutes before serving.
6. Enjoy:

- Serve the BBQ chicken drumsticks hot, garnished with chopped fresh parsley or green onions, if desired.
- They're perfect for a family dinner, backyard barbecue, or game day gathering!

These BBQ chicken drumsticks are sure to be a hit with their smoky flavor and juicy, tender meat. Serve them with your favorite sides like coleslaw, baked beans, or potato salad for a complete meal.

BBQ Pork Belly Burnt Ends

Ingredients:

- 2 lbs pork belly, skin removed and cut into cubes
- BBQ rub or seasoning blend
- BBQ sauce
- Honey or brown sugar (optional, for extra sweetness)

Instructions:

1. Prepare the Pork Belly:
    - Preheat your smoker to 250°F (120°C).
    - Season the pork belly cubes generously with your favorite BBQ rub or seasoning blend, ensuring each piece is coated evenly.
2. Smoke the Pork Belly:
    - Place the seasoned pork belly cubes directly on the smoker rack, leaving some space between each piece for smoke circulation.
    - Smoke the pork belly cubes for 2-3 hours, or until they develop a rich, smoky flavor and have started to render some fat.
3. Wrap and Continue Smoking (optional):
    - If desired, you can wrap the pork belly cubes in aluminum foil or butcher paper after the initial smoking phase to help them retain moisture and tenderness. This step is optional but can help prevent the pork belly from drying out during the cooking process.
4. Glaze with BBQ Sauce:
    - Once the pork belly cubes are fully smoked and tender, remove them from the smoker.
    - Place the cubes in a foil pan or baking dish and generously coat them with BBQ sauce. You can also drizzle some honey or sprinkle brown sugar over the top for extra sweetness, if desired.
5. Return to the Smoker:
    - Place the foil pan or baking dish back on the smoker.
    - Continue to smoke the pork belly cubes for an additional 1-2 hours, or until they are caramelized and sticky, and the sauce has thickened.
6. Serve:
    - Once done, remove the BBQ pork belly burnt ends from the smoker.
    - Allow them to cool for a few minutes before serving.
7. Enjoy:
    - Serve the BBQ pork belly burnt ends as a delicious appetizer or main dish.

- They are perfect for serving at backyard barbecues, tailgate parties, or any occasion when you want to impress your guests with irresistible smoky flavor and tender, caramelized pork belly.

These BBQ pork belly burnt ends are sure to be a hit with anyone who loves rich, savory, and indulgent barbecue dishes. Enjoy the melt-in-your-mouth goodness of these flavorful burnt ends straight from the smoker!

Kansas City BBQ Beef Ribs

Ingredients:

- 2 racks beef ribs (about 4-5 pounds each)
- Kansas City-style BBQ rub or seasoning
- Kansas City-style BBQ sauce
- Wood chips or chunks for smoking (hickory, oak, or pecan)

Instructions:

1. Prep the Ribs:
   - Remove the membrane from the back of the ribs. This helps the rub penetrate the meat better and makes for a more tender end result.
   - Trim any excess fat from the ribs, but leave some for flavor and moisture.
2. Season the Ribs:
   - Season the ribs generously with your Kansas City-style BBQ rub or seasoning blend. Make sure to coat both sides evenly and rub the seasoning into the meat.
3. Preheat the Smoker:
   - Preheat your smoker to 225-250°F (107-121°C). Use wood chips or chunks for smoking, such as hickory, oak, or pecan.
4. Smoke the Ribs:
   - Place the seasoned beef ribs directly on the smoker grate, bone side down.
   - Close the lid and let the ribs smoke for about 4-5 hours, or until they reach an internal temperature of around 200°F (93°C) and the meat is tender and has pulled back from the bones.
5. Glaze with BBQ Sauce:
   - During the last hour of smoking, brush the ribs with Kansas City-style BBQ sauce. Apply multiple layers, allowing each layer to set before applying the next.
6. Rest and Serve:
   - Once the ribs are done, remove them from the smoker and let them rest for about 10-15 minutes before slicing.
   - Slice the ribs between the bones and serve with extra BBQ sauce on the side.
7. Enjoy:
   - Serve the Kansas City BBQ beef ribs hot, and enjoy the flavorful and tender meat with a touch of smoky goodness!

These Kansas City BBQ beef ribs are perfect for any barbecue or cookout, and they're sure to impress your guests with their rich flavor and fall-off-the-bone tenderness. Enjoy the taste of authentic Kansas City barbecue right in your own backyard!

Smoked BBQ Chicken Salad

Ingredients:

- 2 boneless, skinless chicken breasts
- Salt and pepper, to taste
- Your favorite BBQ rub or seasoning blend
- Mixed salad greens (lettuce, spinach, arugula, etc.)
- Cherry tomatoes, halved
- Cucumber, sliced
- Red onion, thinly sliced
- Avocado, sliced
- Corn kernels (fresh, canned, or grilled)
- BBQ sauce, for drizzling
- Ranch dressing or your favorite salad dressing

Instructions:

1. Preheat the Smoker:
    - Preheat your smoker to 225-250°F (107-121°C) using your choice of wood chips or chunks for smoking. Hickory or apple wood works well with chicken.
2. Season the Chicken:
    - Season the chicken breasts generously with salt, pepper, and your favorite BBQ rub or seasoning blend. Make sure to coat both sides evenly.
3. Smoke the Chicken:
    - Place the seasoned chicken breasts directly on the smoker grate.
    - Close the lid and let the chicken smoke for about 1.5 to 2 hours, or until it reaches an internal temperature of 165°F (74°C) and the juices run clear.
4. Shred the Chicken:
    - Once the chicken is done, remove it from the smoker and let it rest for a few minutes.
    - Use two forks to shred the smoked chicken breasts into bite-sized pieces.
5. Assemble the Salad:
    - In a large salad bowl, combine the mixed salad greens, cherry tomatoes, cucumber slices, red onion slices, avocado slices, and corn kernels.
    - Add the shredded smoked BBQ chicken on top of the salad.
6. Drizzle with BBQ Sauce:
    - Drizzle some BBQ sauce over the top of the salad and chicken, to taste.
7. Add Dressing:

- Drizzle ranch dressing or your favorite salad dressing over the salad, to taste.
8. Toss and Serve:
    - Toss the salad gently to combine all the ingredients and evenly coat them with the BBQ sauce and dressing.
    - Serve immediately and enjoy!

This smoked BBQ chicken salad is a delicious and satisfying meal that's perfect for lunch or dinner. It's packed with flavor from the smoked chicken and BBQ sauce, and the combination of fresh vegetables adds crunch and freshness to every bite. Enjoy this tasty salad on its own or alongside your favorite side dishes!

BBQ Pork Tenderloin

Ingredients:

- 1 pork tenderloin (about 1 to 1.5 pounds)
- Salt and pepper, to taste
- 1 tablespoon olive oil
- 1/2 cup BBQ sauce (homemade or store-bought)
- Optional: BBQ rub or seasoning blend

Instructions:

1. Preheat the Grill:
    - Preheat your grill to medium-high heat (about 375-400°F or 190-200°C).
2. Season the Pork Tenderloin:
    - Pat the pork tenderloin dry with paper towels.
    - Season it generously with salt, pepper, and your favorite BBQ rub or seasoning blend. Rub the seasoning into the meat on all sides.
3. Sear the Pork Tenderloin:
    - Heat olive oil in a grill-safe skillet or directly on the grill grates.
    - Once the oil is hot, add the seasoned pork tenderloin to the skillet or grill.
    - Sear the pork tenderloin for 2-3 minutes on each side, or until it develops a nice brown crust.
4. Cook the Pork Tenderloin:
    - Move the seared pork tenderloin to an indirect heat zone on the grill.
    - Close the lid and cook for about 15-20 minutes, or until the internal temperature reaches 145-150°F (63-65°C). Use a meat thermometer to check for doneness.
5. Glaze with BBQ Sauce:
    - During the last 5-10 minutes of cooking, brush the pork tenderloin with BBQ sauce, turning occasionally and brushing with more sauce, until the sauce caramelizes and forms a sticky glaze.
6. Rest and Slice:
    - Once done, remove the pork tenderloin from the grill and let it rest for about 5-10 minutes before slicing. This allows the juices to redistribute and ensures a juicy and tender result.
7. Serve:
    - Slice the BBQ pork tenderloin into thick slices.
    - Serve hot, drizzled with any remaining BBQ sauce from the pan or on the side.

8. Enjoy:
   - Enjoy the juicy and flavorful BBQ pork tenderloin with your favorite sides, such as mashed potatoes, grilled vegetables, or a fresh salad!

This BBQ pork tenderloin recipe is quick and easy to prepare, making it perfect for weeknight dinners or weekend grilling sessions. The combination of savory seasoning and sweet BBQ sauce creates a delicious flavor profile that's sure to be a hit with family and friends.

Kansas City BBQ Chicken Wings

Ingredients:

- 2 lbs chicken wings, split into drumettes and flats
- Salt and pepper, to taste
- Your favorite BBQ rub or seasoning blend
- Kansas City-style BBQ sauce
- Optional: butter or olive oil for basting

Instructions:

1. Preheat the Grill:
    - Preheat your grill to medium-high heat (around 375-400°F or 190-200°C).
2. Season the Wings:
    - Pat the chicken wings dry with paper towels.
    - Season them generously with salt, pepper, and your favorite BBQ rub or seasoning blend. Make sure to coat both sides evenly.
3. Grill the Wings:
    - Place the seasoned chicken wings directly on the grill grates.
    - Grill the wings for about 20-25 minutes, turning occasionally, until they are cooked through and have nice grill marks on all sides.
4. Baste with BBQ Sauce:
    - During the last 5-10 minutes of grilling, brush the chicken wings with Kansas City-style BBQ sauce. Turn them occasionally and brush with more sauce, allowing it to caramelize and form a sticky glaze.
5. Optional Step:
    - For extra flavor and moisture, you can baste the wings with a mixture of melted butter or olive oil and BBQ sauce before serving. This step is optional but adds an extra layer of flavor.
6. Serve:
    - Once the wings are done and glazed with BBQ sauce, remove them from the grill.
    - Transfer the wings to a serving platter and serve hot.
7. Enjoy:
    - Serve the Kansas City BBQ chicken wings with your favorite dipping sauce, such as ranch dressing or blue cheese dressing, and enjoy the delicious combination of smoky, savory, and sweet flavors!

These Kansas City BBQ chicken wings are perfect for serving at parties, game day gatherings, or any occasion when you want to impress your guests with irresistible barbecue flavor. Enjoy them as a tasty appetizer or as part of a larger barbecue feast!

BBQ Beef Brisket Tacos

Ingredients:

- 1 lb beef brisket, cooked and shredded
- Salt and pepper, to taste
- 1 cup BBQ sauce (homemade or store-bought)
- 8-10 small tortillas (flour or corn)
- 1 cup shredded lettuce
- 1 cup diced tomatoes
- 1/2 cup diced red onion
- 1/4 cup chopped fresh cilantro
- Optional toppings: sliced jalapeños, avocado slices, sour cream

Instructions:

1. Prepare the BBQ Beef Brisket:
    - Season the cooked beef brisket with salt and pepper to taste.
    - Shred the brisket using two forks or your hands.
2. Heat the BBQ Sauce:
    - In a small saucepan, heat the BBQ sauce over low heat until warmed through.
3. Assemble the Tacos:
    - Warm the tortillas in a dry skillet or microwave.
    - Place a portion of the shredded BBQ beef brisket onto each tortilla.
    - Top with shredded lettuce, diced tomatoes, diced red onion, and chopped fresh cilantro.
4. Add Optional Toppings:
    - Add sliced jalapeños, avocado slices, or a dollop of sour cream if desired.
5. Drizzle with BBQ Sauce:
    - Drizzle some warmed BBQ sauce over the top of each taco.
6. Serve:
    - Serve the BBQ beef brisket tacos immediately.
7. Enjoy:
    - Enjoy these delicious BBQ beef brisket tacos with your favorite toppings!

These BBQ beef brisket tacos are perfect for a quick and flavorful meal. They're great for weeknight dinners, weekend gatherings, or any occasion when you're craving tasty tacos with a barbecue twist!